STEPS TOWARDS HEAVEN;

OR,

RELIGION IN COMMON LIFE.

A SERIES OF LAY SERMONS FOR CONVERTS IN THE GREAT AWAKENING.

BY T. S. ARTHUR.

NEW YORK:
DERBY & JACKSON, 119 NASSAU STREET.
1858.

W. H. Tinson, Stereotyper.

Geo. Russell & Co., Printers.

PREFACE.

No special theology is taught in this volume. It addresses itself to no particular sect or denomination. It has no aim but to assist men to grow better, and thence, happier. The author comes to the reader, and seeks to inspire him with an unselfish, even a divine and holy purpose; to aid him in the conquest of evil affections; and to furnish him with incentives to right living.

Religion is life; that is, a life of good deeds in the world—and, unless such a life be led, no matter what a man's faith may be, his religion is vain. Piety, which means the formal worship of God, and Charity which consists in acting justly among men, make, when united in any one, the true Christian. Charity is the great essential; for, if a man love not his brother whom he hath seen, how can he love God whom he hath not seen? Worship, therefore, in the absence of charity, is vain, and the prayers of one who does not deal justly and humanely with his fellow-men, can never ascend into heaven.

Such is the doctrine of this book, and in teaching it, the

author has chosen the attractive and beguiling form of life-pictures, narratives, and conversations, hoping thereby to win the attention and hold the interest of his readers, until the lessons he would teach are written upon their minds in ineffaceable characters. He takes, as it were, the truth-seeker at the church door, as he is about going back for his six days' toil, temptation, and experience in the world, and tries to make him comprehend that religion is for the daily life, and cannot be put aside at the tranquil close of Sabbath evenings. That in every department of business; in every office and profession; and in every household duty, men and women must be governed by the divine precepts of the Bible, or they cannot move a step heavenwards, no matter how devoutly they may have worshipped in the congregations of the people.

CONTENTS.

STEPS TOWARDS HEAVEN.

I.

FROM DEATH UNTO LIFE.

The prayer-meeting excitement was over for the day, and Mr. Lyon, who had returned to his family, was feeling the pressure of old states, and the jar of old discordant conditions of life. Mrs. Lyon was weary with her day's work, and manifested an unusual degree of impatience, especially towards the children, whose tempers were altogether out of harmony.

The transition from a prayer-meeting, in which the soul rises into states of ecstasy, or sinks into an almost pulseless tranquillity, to an ill-regulated home, where selfish feelings struggle for the mastery, and discord jars the heart at every pulsation, is very great, and presents one of the strongest trials of a man's religious feelings. He who can meet this change, and yet possess his soul in peace, has, indeed, gained large accessions of spiritual life. There are not many who can pass through the trial unmoved.

"Thank God! Another soul has passed from death unto life!" said a pious brother, as he wrung the hand of Mr. Lyon, on parting with him at the door of the room where the daily prayer-meeting was held. "I greet you as an heir of the Kingdom! You have a goodly heritage. Let me exhort you to stand fast in the faith, and to suffer no man to take your crown."

"I have been near the gate of heaven," Mr. Lyon spoke in a subdued tone, and with a smile of peace on his countenance. "I could almost hear angelic voices—almost see the white garments of the shining ones. Oh, the bliss of heaven! I feel as if I would like to pass upwards, now, to my rest, and be received into the company of saints and martyrs."

"You speak from the warmth of a first love, that is sweeter than honey and the honey-comb," answered the brother. "But we must fight, if we would reign; and you must pray with the poet—

'Increase my courage, Lord.'

"Only they who bear the cross, can wear the crown."

A little dashed were the feelings of Mr. Lyon, by these words of the brother, and he moved on his way homeward, in a less ecstatic frame of mind.

"From death unto life!" The language of congratulation still lingered in his ears. "What death? What life?" These questions a little disturbed him, for the answer was not prompt and clear.

"Born into spiritual life. Born a new creature in God." He uttered the words, mentally, with some firmness, as if to settle the question decisively. But he was not satisfied.

"What is spiritual life? What is a new creature in God? Language that involves such vast concerns can have no vague significance."

Instead of gaining light, the mind of our friend passed into a region of clouds and shadows. He was in this state when he arrived at home. It was just after twilight.

"There now! Father's come!" It was the voice of one of his children, and the tones had in them a threat and a warning.

"I don't care," was the rough, defiant answer.

"He 'll make you care!"

"No he won't!"

"John! Robert! stop this instant!" It was the mother's voice, shrill and jarring. "I won't have your everlasting contention in the house." At this moment, Mrs. Lyon saw her husband; and she went on: "If your father don't do something to put an end to this quarrelling, I'll go off somewhere. I'd rather live in Bedlam!"

What a transition for the young convert! What a fiery test of his new life! The tranquil movement of his sweet emotions was checked, and all the elements of feeling shocked by the sudden jar.

"John! Robert!" Mr. Lyon spoke angrily, for it was as if a sharp spear had pricked him. And he moved towards the boys with an uplifted hand.

"From death unto life." Was it a mocking fiend, or a loving angel, who flung the words into his mind? No matter. The ministry was good. The excited father checked himself, and his hand fell, nerveless, by his side.

"John," he spoke now more in sorrow than in anger, "go into the sitting-room, and you, Robert, remain here. Children who quarrel must be kept apart."

The boys looked curiously at their father, and John obeyed with unusual promptness. There was a new power in Mr. Lyon's voice that left no motion of resistance in the lad's mind.

"Did you order that sugar and butter sent home, as I told you? It hasn't come."

Mrs. Lyon spoke fretfully, and looked at her husband with contracting brows.

"No! I declare I forgot all about it," answered the husband.

"Forgot! Humph! Well, I can tell you; if you want butter on your bread, and sugar in your tea, you've got to go after them now."

Mr. Lyon was not, naturally, of a very amiable disposition, and had never taken, with a good grace, any matrimonial reactions of this kind; so the temptation to answer in as bad a spirit was instant and almost overpowering."

"From death unto life." The thought was just in season. He did not speak, but turned from his companion, and, taking up his hat, went out. In about ten minutes he came back with the needed articles.

"You might have saved yourself that trouble," almost growled Mrs. Lyon. Now, this was too bad; and the repressed feelings of her husband came near blazing out. But, he remembered the prayer-meetings, and his profession, and so strove manfully with the enemies of his peace, that were rushing down upon him like a flood.

At supper time there was little else but discord. The children were, as usual, restless, dissatisfied, and contentious, and their overtried mother—weary in heart and limb—as fretful as she could be. Nor did Mr. Lyon succeed in keeping his own feelings all the while in check. More than once, the inward pressure proved too strong for the outward resistance; and words were said, and acts done,. that were not in harmony with Christian patience.

It is not surprising, that tempting spirits seized upon these occasions, to throw doubt into the young convert's mind, and to suggest that religion was but a cunningly devised fable, and professors only self-deceived, or hypocrites. But there were remains of heavenly truths and holy states, stored up in his mind by a good mother, in the innocent days of childhood and youth, and these were now convictions that no fallacious argument, or false suggestions, could obliterate. Mr. Lyon knew that there was such a thing as spiritual life, and that, when it was born in a human soul, it had power to hold all hell in subjection. And so, though despised, sad and discouraged, he did not abandon the ground he had taken.

After the supper things were removed, the children in bed, the sitting room put in order, and the lamp placed on the centre table, near which Mrs. Lyon sat down with her basket of work, the quieter sphere of the room gave opportunity for the feelings of Mr. Lyon to subside into a more tranquil state. He took the unused family Bible, and laying it upon the centre table, opened it, and after turning over the leaves, commenced reading a chapter aloud.

Mrs. Lyon looked up at her husband curiously, when she saw him take up the family Bible and bring it to the table at which she was sitting. "What does this mean?" she said to herself. When he commenced reading, curiosity gave way to surprise. Mr. Lyon read in a low, impressive voice, the fifth, sixth, and seventh chapters of Matthew, that portion of the Divine Word which is so full of incentives to right living. As he read, the precepts of Him who spake as never man spake, sunk deeply into the hearts of the husband and wife. Into the heart of the husband, because, like a thirsty traveller in a burning desert, he was in search of living waters—into the heart of his wife, because the very novelty of the occasion gave her mind a certain degree of preparation.

After reading these three chapters, Mr. Lyon sat silent and thoughtful for some time.

"There is one thing very certain," said he, at length, "if any man wishes to get to heaven, he must live right in the world."

Mr. Lyon did not address these words to his wife, but uttered them as if speaking to himself. She said nothing, and he remained with his eyes upon the floor.

"Mary." Mrs. Lyon glanced across the table, and met the gaze of her husband. The tone of his voice, and the expression of his eyes, were perceived by her as altogether different from anything she had before observed.

"Mary, I was at a prayer-meeting this afternoon."

"Were you?" Mrs. Lyon seemed interested.

"Yes, Mary." The firmness of tone gave way to a perceptible tremor. "And I think—or hope—that I am a changed man."

A flush of sudden feeling came warmly over the face of Mrs. Lyon.

"Life in this world is short, at best, and very uncertain, Mary, and to make timely preparation for the next is only the dictate of common prudence."

Mrs. Lyon was wholly unprepared for this, and, therefore, her mind was thrown into some confusion. But having broken the ice, so to speak, her husband regained his self-possession, as well as mental clearness. Meeting with no response, he continued:

"I think, Mary, that I am entirely in earnest about this matter. I wish to lead the life of heaven."

Now, Mrs. Lyon had received early religious instruction; and up to the time of her marriage, had been a regular attendant at church. Since her marriage, in consequence of her husband's indifference to spiritual things, she had fallen into a like neglect with him. It was rarely that she attended worship on the Sabbath; and her children were growing up with but few good impressions. Many times had she thought of this; and when early states of mind returned, and she contrasted her own childhood with that of her little ones, painful condemnation would oppress her spirit. "But what can I do?" she would sometimes say to herself. "My husband has no regard for religion." It was but an excuse; yet the excuse prevailed. No wonder this unlooked for announcement bewildered her. She did not answer still; but as Mr. Lyon looked into her eyes, he saw tears filling into them.

"Shall we walk on in this better way, side by side, Mary?" Mr. Lyon spoke with great tenderness, reaching his hand across the table towards the hand of his wife. There was an eager assenting clasp—a sudden bowing of the head—a rain of tears.

"God helping us, we will lead a new life," said Mr. Lyon, breaking in, at last, upon the deep silence.

"There is no help but in Him." Mrs. Lyon looked up, the light of a new hope shining through her tears. "And as I say this," she added, "I remember the words of a preacher, uttered many years ago. They were—'In every good desire God is present, and into every good purpose He flows with strength.' Not in our own strength can we walk in this new way—for it is a heavenly way, and human power is but weakness there. For a divine life, there must be divine strength—and this is the gift of God alone."

Mr. Lyon looked into the face of his wife, wonderingly, as she talked.

"I did not know, Mary, that you had religious views like these," he said. "I thought you were wholly indifferent on the subject."

"No, Henry, not indifferent by any means," she answered, with much earnestness. "My mother was a pious woman, and talked with me about God and heaven, and Christian duty, always. But you never seemed to care about these things; and, gradually, I have fallen into coldness. It seemed to me that the way was too narrow and difficult to walk in alone; and so, I have suffered myself to take the broad, and what appeared the easier, road through the world. But it has not been an easy way in any respect. Something is always getting wrong, and the ground I tread upon each day is rough or miry, though, when seen a little in the distance, it looked smooth and firm as a well beaten path. I am sadly conscious of a steadily growing moral deterioration. I am not as patient, and hopeful, as forbearing and self-denying, as I once was. My temper is less under control. I have wicked, revengeful, and rebellious thoughts. And, most of the time, I am very unhappy. Oh, dear! I shudder often at the image of myself, which seems held up before me as in a mirror. God help me, Henry! I am at times, almost in despair!"

And Mrs. Lyon hid her face in her hands, and wept violently.

"Let me repeat your own words, dear Mary," said her husband. "'For a divine life there must be divine strength, and this is the gift of God alone.' Shall we not pray for it here, and now? His words are, *Ask, and ye shall receive. Seek, and ye shall find. Knock, and it shall be opened unto you.*"

"Here, and now," was the low-murmured answer of Mrs. Lyon.

And so they knelt there together, in this first consecration of themselves; and the husband prayed aloud for wisdom to see the right way, and strength to walk therein.

When they arose from prayer, a deep tranquillity had settled upon their spirits, and their minds seemed elevated into a clearer-seeing region. From the gloom of despondency they had passed into the light of heavenly confidence.

"The language of divine truth is exceedingly plain," said Mr. Lyon, as they sat together. "*Ask, and ye shall receive.* We have asked of our Father in heaven to teach us how to live aright, and he *will* teach us, and lead us in true paths, if we submit as little children. For this we have a thousand assurances, scattered everywhere through the Bible."

"Yes, everywhere," was the subdued answer. "And memory is pointing to precious texts written down upon her tablets long ago. '*Come unto me all ye that labor and are heavy laden, and I will give you rest.*' Does not this seem as if spoken to us now, Henry? It was printed on the first ticket I received in Sunday-school, and is as fresh in my thought now as then. Oh! is it not full of comfort and hope? '*Come unto me.*' 'I *will* give you rest.' There is no qualification; no discrimination. *All* who labor and are heavy laden."

"God has changed our hearts," said Mr. Lyon, warming into enthusiasm. "We have passed from death into life. We are dead to sin, and alive in Christ Jesus our Lord. Blessed be God for his divine grace, that cleanses from all defilements!"

"From death unto life?" Mrs. Lyon looked almost soberly into her husband's face.

"Is it not so?" he questioned. "Dead to sin, and alive to righteousness?"

"God grant that it *may* be so," was the quiet answer. "But the hard duties of life are before us, Henry; and more—" She paused, with almost a sad countenance.

"More? Say on, Mary."

"We may be dead to sin. I pray heaven that it be so. But, whatever of new life may be born within us from God, must be feeble as the babe's life. And, with only this feeble life to sustain us, we have to do battle with the strong man of evil."

"But God is on our side. In his strength we can overcome all our enemies," said Mr. Lyon.

"If we will but look to Him in the hour of temptation."

"We must—we must. There is no other hope." Mr. Lyon's enthusiasm was dying down. He saw that there was not only work, but a battle before them, and that they must toil and fight, if they would come off victorious.

On the next morning, the calm, sober, earnest manner of Mr. and Mrs. Lyon had a marked effect upon their badly trained children, who at once observed the change, and waited, curiously, to see just what it meant.

"Will you hand me the Bible, Mary?" said Mr. Lyon, speaking to his wife, as she came into the room where he was sitting with the children, to say that breakfast was ready.

She looked at him for a moment, almost wonderingly, and then, with an assenting smile, lifted the family Bible from a stand, and placing it before him, sat down by his side. The children gazed, curiously, at both their father and mother, and waited in silence for what was to succeed. A chapter was read, in a low, serious voice. Then the father and mother knelt down, and the children did likewise. The prayer was brief, just covering the needs and experience of the petitioner. There were no vain words, nor any pompous phraseology; but a humble directness, that showed an earnest heart.

For the first time, in months, Mr. and Mrs. Lyon enjoyed a quiet, orderly meal. The effect of this unlooked-for act of worship, was to subdue the children's minds, as well as to excite their curiosity; and as the parents maintained a calm, rather sober demeanor, they yielded to the new influence, and took an altogether improved exterior.

"There is a wonderful power in divine grace," said Mr. Lyon, as he was parting with his wife, after breakfast. "It has subdued even these almost ungovernable children." He spoke with a glow of enthusiasm.

Mrs. Lyon did not respond; but looked into his face earnestly, and with eyes that had in them a shade of sadness.

"Is the whispering Doubter already at your ear, Mary?" The husband spoke almost in reproof.

"It is he that *overcometh*, who shall not be hurt of the second death," said Mrs. Lyon.

"Through God strengthening me, I can do all things." Mr. Lyon spoke with renewed enthusiasm.

A faint smile went over the face of his wife.

"Is it not so? Have we not the sure word of promise?"

"Yes, and I believe it," was the low, sober, almost sad response.

"Then why are you cast down, Mary? Have faith in God. Trust him—look to him. He is stronger than all our enemies."

"All this is well to be said, Henry; for it is true, and gives strength and hope. But Christian graces are given, not as ornaments, but as tools for work, and armor for battle. Religion is life—that is, a good life; and the life cannot be good, unless the acts are good. And now abideth faith, hope, and charity, these three; but the greatest of these is charity. Faith is idle, and hope vain, unless they subside in charity. So I read the divine law."

"Look up, Mary. Pray for strength—pray without ceasing," said Mr. Lyon encouragingly. "God *will* give you strength for duty."

"I must watch, and work, and guard, as well as pray," was answered. "There will be sudden assaults upon my patience, and untimely demands on my discretion. In a moment of weariness, or exhaustion, sharp provocations to anger will come. When thought acts feebly, because both mind and body are overstrained, there will arise some pressing need for wisdom and prudence. Can I hope always to be patient and discreet, wise and prudent? No, Henry; that is impossible. But, God helping me, I will do my best. I cannot rise into these new-born ecstasies. I do not see the Christian life as one of undiminished sunshine and heavenly tranquillity. There must be conquest, ere smiling peace is born; there must be night, ere the glad morning breaks; labor, before rest. *Well done good and faithful* SERVANT, are the words of welcome into heaven."

"God will help you, Mary," was Mr. Lyon's softened reply. "I see that you are indeed in earnest; that you mean to begin right. Let me say this to encourage you—it comes but now into my thought. After *every* conquest, will come a state of peace; after *every* night of fear and doubt, a sunny morning; after *every* period of labor, rest. And so, with the daily trial, will come the daily blessing."

"Thank you, dear husband," said Mrs. Lyon, a gleam of light shooting across her face; "I just needed that. Now I see clearer. Now I feel a higher strength."

They parted for the day. We cannot follow them through its varied scenes, nor show how their new-born faith was tried. They had helped each other by mutual suggestions, and did not, therefore, go into the new life-battle with any vain confidence. If God gave the power to fight against evil, they saw that they must use it as if it were their own; that a change of purpose was not a change in any of the laws of the soul's being. The individual must overcome, if he would triumph. All that God did for him was to supply proof-armor, a sword, and strength. Beyond that, all rested with himself. There was hope for them; as there is for all who see the way clearly, and are in earnest to walk therein.

Not light had been the trials, nor feeble the assaults of evil, which Mr. Lyon endured through the day, and when he turned his steps homeward at its close, he was in a soberer mood than when he left the prayer-meeting on the evening before. Husband and wife looked into each other's faces earnestly when they met. Faint smiles, that soon faded, played about their quiet lips. But there were deep meanings in their eyes, that seemed to have grown clearer and calmer. Mr. Lyon did not find a storm, nor even the evidences of a storm. Instead of being engaged in quarrelling, John was doing something for his mother, and Robert sat reading. There was an unusual stillness in the house, and evidences of a new order of things all around. A neater set tea-table he had not seen for a long time than the one he found in the little dining-room, nor had his food tasted so sweet for years.

After the children were in bed, and the father and mother were alone together again, Mr. Lyon leaned across the little centre-table on which the lamp had been placed, and looked steadily into the face of his wife, who sat on the other side.

"How has the day passed, Mary?" he asked.

Mrs. Lyon did not smile, as she looked up and met her husband's eyes.

"Well?"

"Better than I had hoped; yet I cannot say well," she answered, soberly.

"I can see the evidences of a great and a good work, well begun," was the encouraging answer of Mr. Lyon. "How singularly quiet and readily obedient the children were. The mother's hand is in this."

"You have seen them in their best condition," Mrs. Lyon replied. "It has not been so through all the day. I have had to watch them with the closest care, and to judge of them and between them, when it seemed as if my over-tried spirit was losing its power to see and to act. I have learned one good lesson in the trial. There must be self-control and self-conquest, before we can hope to subdue evil in others. Just in the degree that I was able to control myself, was I able to govern the children, and to subdue them to my will. But, if I spoke with the slightest sign of anger, my words seemed lost in the empty air."

"Then there has been a double victory over the powers of evil," said Mr. Lyon, with a smile of pleasure glowing in his face. "A victory on the battle field of your own heart, and a victory in the strife with our children."

"I can scarcely call it a victory in my own case," was answered. "I was only not driven from the field."

It was a long time since, in the eyes of Mr. Lyon, the face of his wife had worn an aspect so pleasing as now. He gazed upon it in almost loving wonder.

"Are you discouraged, Mary?" he asked.

"Discouraged? Oh, no!" Her countenance brightened suddenly. "Do you think I have forgotten the hopeful sentence you gave me this morning. 'After every conquest will come a state of peace—after every night of doubt and fear, a sunny morning—after every period of labor, rest. And so, with the daily trial will come the daily blessing.' No, no; and now, dear husband! after this brief period of strife, darkness, and labor, I have a measure of tranquillity, light, and rest. The daily trial is past, and I have the blessing."

"And the blessing is worth all that it has cost," said Mr. Lyon.

"All, and more than all," she quickly answered. "This, Henry, is, indeed, the better way, and my heart is full of thankfulness, that our feet have turned aside and entered its narrow bounds. And it is easier to walk herein than I had believed. We have but to make the effort to move forward, and God gives instant strength. The lion standing with fierce aspect a little in the distance, terrifies us with his threatening roar; but as we approach, putting our confidence in Heaven, we see the chain that holds him, powerless for harm. If some enemy to our peace make a sudden and malignant assault, we have but to lift the sword-bearing arm, and more than a giant's strength flows in from heaven. It is not a vain thing to put our trust in God. But, tell me of your day's experiences, Henry. How has this new life sustained you?"

The eyes of Mr. Lyon fell slowly to the floor: a shadow dimmed his face; a sigh troubled his bosom.

"I am afraid, Mary," he answered, after some

moments, that, but, for your more practical view, of this question of religion, I should be lower down in the valley of discouragement than I am now. I came home last evening, in a kind of ecstatic condition of mind, and with only vague notions touching the new life I had resolved to lead. The first shock of our disorderly home staggered me. The transition of feeling was from glowing heat to sudden cold. I was bewildered, and, for a time, in almost hopeless discouragement. But, I was really in earnest, and, following the way on which fell some feeble gleams of light, and acting upon some new born impulses from Heaven, I compelled myself to open the long unused Bible, and to read aloud, not knowing how you would act, or what you would say. Oh, Mary! When you turned to me in the right spirit, my heart leaped upwards, as if a crushing weight had been suddenly removed. Then, as we conversed, I found your perceptions going right down to the bottom of the whole question of religion, as a matter of self-conquest and right living; and you lifted my reason up into just conclusion. So we helped, and encouraged one another. I saw, that, if indeed, I had passed, as some say, from death unto life, I was not a strong man, but, an almost helpless infant, and that growth and development were as necessary to my spiritual manhood, as to the manhood of natural and rational life. All day long I have been thinking over that matter of the new birth, Mary, and I am sure, taking the experiences of this day as conclusive on the subject, that, but for the help you afforded me last night, I should have given way to overwhelming doubts. I found, when any evil allurement came, that evil desire was not extinguished; only, that a desire for the opposite good was born. If you had not helped me to think of the new birth as only the first beginning of a spiritual state, I would have, I fear, abandoned all as a delusion; for, if I were really a new creature in Christ Jesus—if I had passed from death unto life—taking these things in their broader meanings—how could I still have evil desires? But light came, and strength with light. If good impulses were very feeble, yet, when I looked up, and made an effort to do right, help came. Sometimes I was taken off my guard, and stricken down in a moment. But, at that point I placed a sentinel. So you see that I have been at work in good earnest—though little has been done. I do not feel greatly encouraged; and yet, hope rests on a strong foundation. Reason appreciates and judgment approves the mode of regeneration, that seem to me like steps towards a mountain height, or ascending spirals, gradually bearing the soul upwards to heaven."

"His Word," said Mrs. Lyon, reverently, as her husband paused, "shall be a lamp unto our feet, and a light unto our path. I think we have begun right. God sees the desire of our hearts, and will give us the needed strength in every time of trial. We will look to him in prayer, and in his Holy Word; and He will not hide from us the light of his countenance. Your day's experience is like my own; and if in anything I happened to say, you found strength, I must own that from your fitly spoken suggestions, came to me a world of aid and comfort. Without them, I think I must have fallen by the way."

How much depends on a right beginning. We see it in this single day's experience of two who had resolved to lead the life of heaven—a life, not of mere feeling, but of doing. Not of pious acts and the formal worship of the sanctuary alone, but a life of daily self-denial and good deeds. They had begun right, adding, to prayer and faith, effort—meeting temptation with the armor on, and battling for the victory. They had, indeed, passed from death unto life; and though only yet, as it were, babes in Christ, the first fruits of the new birth were plainly visible. Of such is the kingdom of heaven.

Few of those who begin the Christian pilgrimage in a like spirit ever turn aside, or go back again into their old ways. Every step is an advance in the regenerate life; every strife with the powers of hell gives strength or victory; every night of temptation, but precedes the surely coming dawn of a brighter day. Religion, to be of any real use to a man, must come down into all his daily duties, and regulate his actions by a divine standard. It must make him patient, thoughtful of others, self-denying, watchful against evil, and, above all, just in even the smallest things, towards his fellow-man. For, no matter how externally pious a man may be; no matter how faithfully he may attend upon the ordinances of the church; if he love not his neighbor, he cannot have God's love in his heart, and all who think and act differently are yielding to a fatal delusion.

II.

AS WE FORGIVE.

"He must pay it." The voice that said this was firm, and the tone decided.

"I think he is very poor, Mr. Glenn," answered the collector, who was making his weekly return.

"No matter; poor people must pay their debts as well as rich ones. I can't undertake to supply the family of every poor man in the city with shoes. There wouldn't be a pair left for my own children's feet, if I undertook such a piece of Quixotic benevolence."

And Mr. Glenn smiled a little grimly, as if there were something of humor in the closing sentence.

"It strikes me that there is an exception in this case," remarked the collector.

"None at all—none at all," replied the dealer in boots and shoes. "Poor people must be honest as well as rich ones, and not buy more than they are able to pay for. Horton must settle. There is no use in his trying to shirk out of it."

"He has been sick."

"Well, what of that? Other poor men are not exempt from sickness. It is the common lot. Let him do something, if it is ever so little, and thus show an honest disposition."

"It is hard to do something with nothing," said the collector.

"How does he live? He eats and drinks, doesn't he?" interrogated Mr. Glenn.

"I suppose so, and his wife and children also."

"Does he steal the money he lives on?"

"I didn't investigate the case that far," replied the collector, showing a little annoyance.

"He earns it, no doubt. And there is one thing I have to say in the matter—while Horton is in debt he has no right to spend all he earns. He should pay off something, if it is ever so small a portion, of what is due to others. That is being simply honest."

"He has four little children; his wife is in bad health, and he is working on three-quarter time. I am sure, Mr. Glenn, that he cannot, as things now are, pay anything on your bill, without actually diminishing the supply of food, or being turned out of house and home.

"Oh! he pays his rent, then, does he?"

"He said that his landlord was a very close man, and required the rent weekly. That he had got a little behindhand with him, and was compelled not only to pay up the current rent, but a certain sum on what was due, at the same time, or have his things put into the street."

"I see. He will pay only on compulsion. If that is his game, we will accommodate him. Just call and say, that unless he shows some disposition to settle, that I will send a constable after him."

"I wouldn't take that course, Mr. Glenn. His intentions are honest, I am certain. But things have gone wrong with him, and he is very much under the weather."

"Good intentions don't save any one. There must be good deeds. Nothing else will pass current here, or hereafter. Let Horton show his honest purpose by beginning to do honest acts. Nothing less will satisfy me. Can't he pay twenty-five cents a week?"

"He might do so, I presume."

"Very well, let him begin at that figure. Tell

him that so long as he pays twenty-five cents a week, punctually, I will not disturb him; but on the first failure he may expect to see the constable."

"I must decline being the bearer of that message," replied the collector. "I would rather pay twenty-five cents a week out of my own pocket, than be your agent in any such business."

The face of Mr. Glenn grew red with anger, and he said, sharply—

"I want none of your reflections on my acts or purposes. As you have undertaken my collections, I wish the work done as I direct. The responsibility rests with me."

"Take my advice," returned the collector coolly, "and forgive this poor man his debt. It amounts to only seven dollars, and its loss will not deprive you of a single comfort, while the act will relieve him from a heavy burden. He is honest; and will pay you, if it is ever in his power, whether you cancel the obligation or not."

"You are generous with what is not your own," said Glenn, with sarcasm. "Thank you for the suggestion; but I am not in the habit of trusting people and then forgiving them the debt. That sort of thing doesn't pay."

"It does in some cases," remarked the collector, speaking partly to himself.

"It will not pay in this, for I don't mean to try the foolish experiment," answered Glenn.

Turning towards this hard man, who was a member of one of the churches, the collector—who was also a church-member, but of a different stamp—looked him steadily in the face for some moments, and then said

"When you kneel before God this evening, and, in praying, say over the words, 'Forgive us our debts *as* we forgive our debtors,' take heed that you are not asking for a curse instead of a blessing. If God forgives you *as* you now forgive this poor man, the case will not assume a very hopeful aspect. '*But if ye forgive not men their trespasses, neither will your Father forgive your trespasses.*' The language is not mine; I but recall to your memory the words of eternal truth. Beware, lest, knowing these, you have the greater condemnation."

Saying this, the collector turned away, and left Mr. Glenn to his own not very pleasant thoughts.

That evening, in family worship, Mr. Glenn said over the Lord's Prayer. If the collector had been present, he would have observed a faltering in the words, "*As we forgive our debtors.*" He had never before understood them as now, though he had repeated these words a thousand times since they were taught to him by his mother in childhood. All at once they had assumed a new and startling significance. 'Forgive us our debts *as* we forgive our debtors!' Here was no vague petition, but a plain request to be dealt by as the petitioner dealt by his neighbor. '*With what measure ye meet, it shall be measured to you again.*" The memory of this passage, also, grew quite distinct in the mind of Mr. Glenn, and it seemed also as if spoken aloud in his ears. Conscience was at work, and fear troubling him.

"What if my soul should be required of me this night?" A sudden shiver ran through his nerves as this thought presented itself.

"God has heard and answered some of my prayers," said Mr. Glenn, as he sat apart from his family, pondering this new aspect of the case. "I asked Him, at the outset of life, to be with me in my incomings and outgoings; to smile upon my toil, and send the rain of prosperity upon my fields. And he has done so. I have prayed also from childhood, onward to this time, that he would forgive me my debts *as* I forgiven my debtors. Now, have I ever, in my heart, forgiven the man who trespassed against me? or refrained from exacting from a debtor the last farthing, no matter what his needs and circumstances? Have I regarded my brother in sickness or misfortune? Has pity touched my soul, when the unhappy debtor has pleaded for respite or forgiveness? Should God answer my oft-repeated prayer in this, will it not be in banishment from his presence?"

For hours that night, Mr. Glenn lay tossing on his bed, fearing to sleep, lest his awakening should be in another world; but, wearied nature yielded at last, and then in visions of his bed, he closed up his mortal career, and passed to his final account. But, no "Well done, good and faithful servant greeted him!" Instead there burned before him in letters of flame, turn which way he would—"With what measure ye mete, it shall be measured to you again." He closed his eyes—"As we forgive our debtors," were gleaming in their place, though he tried to shut out the vision of all things. In terrible anguish he awoke. Again he slept, and the vision was repeated. And once again, ere the day broke.

Mr. Glenn assembled his household for morning worship as usual; and read a chapter from the Bible. His voice was low, and humble. The petition that followed was brief; and members of his family noticed, as an unusual thing, that he failed to conclude with the Lord's Prayer. His first act, on going to his store, was to send Mr. Horton, the poor debtor for whom the humane collector had pleaded, a receipt in full, thus cancelling the debt. He felt more comfortable after this; but still, a weight of concern lay upon his heart. Here was a new reading of the Divine precept, and one that, if accepted, might, he feared, require a degree of sacrifice that, in the present state of his natural affections, he could not give. The law, as narrowing itself down to his most literal rendering of the text, seemed the hardest in the whole code of Divine precepts.

But, Mr. Glenn had begun right. If we constrain ourselves to do what we believe the law of God requires, we always gain power over depraving lusts, and selfish affections. We must fight against the powers of hell, or there will be no conquest. We must put away evil, before angelic loves can flow into our hearts. The case of Mr. Glenn is an illustration. The reader has seen how hard and cruel were all his feelings towards his poor debtor. Not a single wave of pity moved over his heart—not a pulse of commiseration stirred. It was different however, after he had so far conquered his selfish desire for gain, as to cancel the debt. Then pity for Horton began to work in his heart, and draw before his imagination images of sickness, discouragement, privation and suffering.

"Poor man! He has had a hard time of it. I am glad that I lifted that burden from his shoulders," he said to himself in this great change of state.

And now, the current of feeling which was flowing in the right direction, began to set stronger. Pity is not a mere idler; but a door of good deeds. Mr. Glenn began to feel an interest in the poor man, which led him to make particular inquiry into his circumstances. He found that help was really needed, and with a cheerful alacrity that surprised even himself, he reached out his hand to raise up and sustain a weak and falling brother. It was the beginning of a new life for Mr. Glenn, and one in which this small experience showed him were new and higher pleasures than any he had ever known—the pleasures that always accompany good deeds lovingly performed.

Some weeks passed, before he again ventured to say the Lord's Prayer, in family worship. But, when the petition did pass his lips, it was in the humble hope that God would give him that spirit of forgiveness, without which there can be no remission of sins.

III.

HEAVENLY-MINDED.

I LISTENED while he talked in a low, serious, tender voice. He was speaking of the home in heaven towards which his heart aspired.

"There will be no more night there, nor chilling winter," he said; "no more sorrow, no more toil, no more pain; for God is the light of that world, and he will wipe away all tears from our eyes. How often do I find myself crying out with the Psalmist, 'Oh that I had wings like a dove, for then would I fly away, and be at rest!' I grow weary with waiting every day. This world has no attractions to offer my soul. Its atmosphere oppresses me; its ways are rough to my feet; its touch chills me. I pray continually, O Lord, hide me under the shadow of thy wings, until the storms of life are over; shelter me from the burning heats; cover me from the winter's cold."

And then he sang in a sweet, impressive way—

"Jerusalem, my happy home!
Oh, how I long for thee.
When will my sorrows have an end?
Thy joys when shall I see?"

"How heavenly-minded!" I heard spoken from one to another, in a hushed whisper.

"He is ripe for the kingdom," was answered back.

"The world hangs loosely upon him as a worn-out garment, ready to be cast aside when the Master summons him away. God has endowed him with a double portion of his Spirit."

I walked thoughtfully away when the little company separated. "Is it indeed so?" I questioned with myself. 'Heavenly-minded?' 'Ripe for the kingdom?' 'A double portion of God's Spirit resting upon him?" What is it to be heavenly-minded? How is a man ripened for the kingdom of God?"

I knew a little of the man's past and present. He had not been an earnest worker in the world; but, rather, an idler and a dreamer. He was something of an enthusiast, and had the reputation of being "gifted in prayer." He talked much on the subject of religion, and spent a great deal of time in preparing himself for heaven. This preparation consisted, mainly, in pious observances, the reading of religious books, fasting and prayer. In business, he had not succeeded, because he lacked earnestness, prudence, and industry. There was, to his perception, a spirit of worldly-mindedness in these, opposed to religion. It was a letting of himself down into carnal things, that were death to the spiritn. Ad so he was very poor, and could sing, and did sing, with feeling—

"No foot of land do I possess,
Nor cottage in the wilderness—
A poor, way-faring man.
I lodge, awhile, in tents below,
Or gladly wander to and fro,
Till I my Canaan gain."

And rather took merit to himself for his poverty; regarding it almost as one of the Christian graces.

I need hardly say, that the wife of this man was a toiler beyond her strength, and that his children had not received the natural and moral advantages that their father might have procured for them, if he had been a worker in the world, instead of an enthusiastic dreamer. The burdens of others were made heavier, because he had failed to bear his own allotment; and evil had crept in at the door he was appointed to guard, because he had slept at his post. And yet he was called "heavenly-minded," and ripe for the kingdom.

As I mused, reason and feeling both demurred. I could see nothing of the spirit of heaven in this; but only the delusion of an unprofitable servant. To be heavenly-minded, is to be in the love of good deeds; and every man who, from a religious principle, acts justly and faithfully in all his relations in life, is a doer of good deeds. He only can become heavenly-minded; he only can worship God in spirit and in truth. Praying and singing are of no avail, without acting. They may lift the thoughts heavenward; but only as our feet move are we borne thitherward. We are in the world for work and duty; and we cannot be righteous, unless we act right towards our fellow-men. Belief in God, and an acknowledgment of his holy precepts, are only as the inception of spiritual life; true vitality and Christian manhood are the results of right living. It is the good and faithful servant who alone enters into the joy of his Lord; only he who performs good acts to the children of men is accepted.

It is easier to pray than to work; easier to believe a certain formula, than to practise self-denial; easier to permit the feelings to lapse sweetly away under the influence of tranquillizing music, than to compel self-love to give up its darling scheme. But only in the degree that we overcome the man of sin, who is ever prompting to a disregard of others, that we may get larger worldly benefits and increased natural enjoyments, do we receive true spiritual life, and advance in the way of regeneration. To rest a hope of heaven on any other ground, is a most fatal delusion.

IV.

WHEAT OR TARES.

"WHEAT or tares—which are you sowing, Fanny, dear, in the mind of this sweet little fellow?" said Uncle Lincoln to his niece, Mrs. Howard, as he lifted a child not yet beyond his fourth summer upon his knee, and laid one of his hands amid the golden curls that fell about his neck, and clustered above his snowy temples.

"Wheat, I trust, Uncle Lincoln," replied Mrs. Howard, smiling, yet serious. "It is the enemy who sows tares—and I am his mother."

There was a glow of proud feeling in the countenance of Mrs. Howard, as she said, "I am his mother."

It was Mr. Lincoln's first visit to his niece since her marriage and removal to the city, some hundreds of miles away from her old home.

"Even a mother's hand may sow tares," said the

old gentleman. "I have seen it done many times. Not of design, but in thoughtless inattention to the quality of the seed she holds in her hand. The enemy mixes tares with the wheat, quite as often as he scatters evil seed. The husbandman must not only watch his fields by night and by day, but also the repositories of his grain, lest the enemy cause him to sow tares as well as wheat upon his own fruitful ground."

"Willie," said Mrs. Howard, speaking to her little boy about ten minutes afterwards, "don't upset my work-basket. Stop! Stop, I say, you little rogue!"

Seeing that the wayward child did not mean to heed her words, the mother started forwards, but not in time to prevent the spools of cotton, scissors, needles, emery-cushion, etc., from being scattered about the floor.

Willie laughed in great glee at his exploit, while Mrs. Howard gathered up the contents of the work-basket, which she now placed on a shelf above the reach of her mischievous boy. Then she shook her finger at him in mock resentment, saying—

"You little sinner! If you do that again, I'll send you off with the milkman."

"Wheat or tares, Fanny?" Uncle Lincoln looked soberly at his niece.

"Neither," replied Mrs. Howard, smiling gayly.

"Tares," said Uncle Lincoln, emphatically.

"Nonsense, uncle!"

"The tares of disobedience, Fanny. You have planted the seed, and it has already taken root. Nothing will choke out the wheat sooner. The tares of falsehood you also threw in upon the newly-broken soil. What are you thinking about, my child?"

"The tares of falsehood, Uncle Lincoln! What are *you* thinking about?" said Mrs. Howard, in real surprise.

"Did you not say that you would send him off with the milkman if he did so again? I wonder if he believed you?"

"Of course he did not."

"Then," said Uncle Lincoln, "he has already discovered that his mother makes but light account of truth. Will his mother be surprised if he should grow to set small value upon his word?"

"You treat the matter too seriously, uncle. He knows that I am only playing with him."

"He knows that you are telling him what is not true," replied Mr. Lincoln.

"It was only in sport," said Fanny, persistently.

"But in sport with sharp-edged instruments—playing with deadly poisons." The old gentleman looked and spoke with the seriousness that oppressed his feelings. "Fanny! Fanny! Truth and obedience are good seeds; falsehood and disobedience are tares from the Evil One. Whatever you plant in the garden of your child's mind will grow, and the harvest will be wheat or tares, just as you have sown."

Mrs. Howard did not reply, but her countenance took on a sober cast.

"Willie," said she, a few minutes afterwards, "go down to Jane and tell her to bring me a glass of water."

Willie, who was amusing himself with some pictures, looked up on hearing his name. But as he did not feel like going off to the kitchen, he made no response, and let his eyes return to the pictures, in which he had become interested.

"Willie (Mrs. Howard spoke with decision), "did you hear me?"

"I don't want to go," answered Willie.

"Go this minute!"

"I'm afraid."

"Go, I say!"

"I'm afraid."

"Afraid of what?" inquired the mother.

"Afraid of the cat."

"No, you are not. The cat never hurt you, nor any body else."

"I'm afraid of the milkman. You said he should carry me off."

"The milkman is not down stairs," said Mrs. Howard, her face beginning to crimson; "he only comes in the morning."

"Yes, he is. I heard his wagon a little while ago, and he's talking with Jane now. Don't you hear him?" the little fellow put on, with remarkable skill, all the semblances of truth in his tone and expression.

Mrs. Howard did not look towards her uncle; she was afraid to do that.

"Willie," (the mother spoke very seriously), "you know the milkman is not down stairs; and you know that you are not afraid of the cat. What you have said, therefore, is not true; and it is wicked to utter a falsehood."

"Ho! ho!" laughed out the bright-eyed little fellow, evidently amused at his own sharpness, "then you're wicked, for you tell what is not true every day."

"Willie!"

"The milkman hasn't carried me off yet!"

There was a world of meaning in Willie's countenance and voice.

You hav'n't whipped me for throwing my cap out of the window."

"Willie!" ejaculated the astonished mother.

"D'ye see that?" and the young rebel drew from his apron pocket a fine mosaic breast-pin, which he had positively been forbidden to touch, and held it up with a look of mingled triumph and defiance.

"You little wretch!" exclaimed Mrs. Howard; "this is going too far!" and springing towards her boy, she grappled him in her arms, and fled with him, struggling from the room.

It was a quarter of an hour before she returned, alone, to the apartment where she had left her uncle. Her face was sober, and her eyes betrayed recent tears.

"Wheat or tares, Fanny?" said the old gentleman, in kind but earnest tones, as his niece came back.

"Tares," was the half-mournful response.

"Wheat were better, Fanny."

"I see it, uncle."

And you will look well in future to the seed in your hand, ere you scatter it upon the heart of your child."

"God helping me, I will, dear uncle."

"Remember, Fanny," said Mr. Lincoln, "that truth and obedience are good seed. Plant them, and the harvest-time will come in blessing. As a Christian mother, this is one of your highest and most sacred duties. God has given you a child that you may raise him for heaven; and he has furnished you with an abundant supply of the precious seeds of love, truth, tenderness, and mercy to sow in his mind. Oh, scatter them broadcast over the rich soil prepared to receive them, and they will take root, spring up, and bear an abundance of good fruit in the harvest-time of his life."

V.

IS HE A CHRISTIAN?

"Is he a Christian?

The question reached my ear as I sat conversing with a friend, and I paused in the sentence I was uttering, to note the answer.

"Oh, yes; he is a Christian," was replied.

"I am rejoiced to hear you say so. I was not aware of it before," said the other.

"Yes; he has passed from death unto life. Last week, in the joy of his new birth, he united himself to the church, and is now in fellowship with the saints."

"What a blessed change!"

"Blessed, indeed. Another soul saved; another added to the great company of those who have washed their robes, and made them white, in the blood of the Lamb. There is joy in heaven on his account."

"Of whom are they speaking?" I asked, turning to my friend.

"Of Fletcher Gray, I believe," was replied.

"Few men stood more in need of Christian graces," said I. "If he is, indeed, numbered with the saints, there is cause for rejoicing."

"By their fruits ye shall know them," responded my friend. "I will believe his claim to the title of Christian, when I see the fruit in good living. If he have truly passed from death unto life, as they say, he will work the works of righteousness. A sweet fountain will not send forth bitter waters."

My friend but expressed my own sentiments in this, and all like cases. I have learned to put small trust in "profession;" to look past the Sunday and prayer-meeting piety of people, and to estimate religious quality by the standard of the Apostle James. There must be genuine love of the neighbor, before there can be a love of God; for neighborly love is the ground in which that higher and purer love takes root. It is all in vain to talk of love as a mere ideal thing. Love is an active principle, and, according to its quality, works. If the love be heavenly, it will show itself in good deeds to the neighbor; but, if infernal, in acts of selfishness that disregard the neighbor.

"I will observe this Mr. Gray," said I, as I walked homeward from the company, "and see whether the report touching him be true. If he is, indeed, a 'Christian,' as they affirm, the Christian graces of meekness and charity will blossom in his life, and make all the air around him fragrant."

Opportunity soon came. Fletcher Gray was a storekeeper, and his life in the world was, consequently, open to the observation of all men. He was likewise a husband and a father. His relations were, therefore, of a character to give, daily, a test of his true quality.

It was only the day after, that I happened to meet Mr. Gray under circumstances favorable to observation. He came into the store of a merchant with whom I was transacting some business, and asked the price of certain goods in the market. I moved aside, and watched him narrowly. There was a marked change in the expression of his countenance and in the tones of his voice. The former had a sober, almost solemn expression; the latter was subdued, even to plaintiveness. But, in a little while, these peculiarities gradually disappeared, and the aforetime Mr. Gray stood there unchanged—unchanged, not only in appearance, but in character. There was nothing of the "yea, yea," and "nay, nay," spirit in his bargain-making, but an eager, wordy effort to gain an advantage in trade. I noticed that, in the face of an asseveration that only five per cent. over cost was asked for a certain article, he still endeavored to procure it at a lower figure than was named by the seller, and finally crowded him down to the exact cost, knowing, as he did, that the merchant had a large stock on hand and could not well afford to hold it over.

"He's a sharper!" said the merchant, turning towards me as Gray left the store.

"He's a Christian, they say," was my quiet remark.

"A Christian!"

"Yes; don't you know that he has become religious, and joined the church?"

"You're joking!"

"Not a word of it. Didn't you observe his subdued, meek aspect, when he came in?"

"Why, yes; now that you refer to it, I do remember a certain peculiarity about him. Become pious! Joined the church! Well, I'm sorry!"

"For what?

"Sorry for the injury he will do to a good cause. The religion that makes a man a better husband, father, man of business, lawyer, doctor, or preacher, I reverence, for it is genuine, as the lives of those who accept it do testify. But your hypocritical pretenders I scorn and execrate."

"It is, perhaps, almost too strong language this, as applied to Mr. Gray," said I.

"What is a hypocrite?" asked the merchant.

"A man who puts on the semblance of Christian virtues which he does not possess."

"And that is what Mr. Gray does when he assumes to be religious. A true Christian is just. Was he just to me when he crowded me down in the price of my goods, and robbed me of a living profit, in order that he might secure a double gain? I think not. There is not even the live and let live principle in that. No—no, sir. If he has joined the church, my word for it, there is a black sheep in the fold; or, I might say, without abuse of language, a wolf therein, disguised in sheep's clothing."

"Give the man time," said I. "Old habits of life are strong, you know. In a little while, I trust that he will see clearer, and regulate his life from perceptions of higher truths."

"I thought his heart was changed," answered the merchant, with some irony in his tones. "That he had been made a new creature."

I did not care to discuss that point with him, and so merely answered.

"The beginnings of spiritual life, are as the beginnings of natural life. The babe is born in feebleness, and we must wait through the periods of infancy, childhood, and youth, before we can have the strong man ready for the burden and heat of the day, or full-armed for the battle. If Mr. Gray is in the first effort to lead a Christian life, that is something. He will grow wiser and better in time, I hope."

"There is vast room for improvement," said the merchant. "In my eyes, he is, at this time, only a hypocritical pretender. I hope, for the sake of the world and the church both, that his new associates will make something better out of him."

I went away, pretty much of the merchant's opinion. My next meeting with Mr. Gray was in the shop of a mechanic to whom he had sold a bill of goods some months previously. He had called to collect a portion of the amount which remained unpaid. The mechanic was not ready for him.

"I am sorry, Mr. Gray," he began, with some hesitation of manner.

"Sorry for what?" sharply interrupted Mr. Gray.

"Sorry that I have not the money to settle your bill. I have been disappointed——"

"I don't want that old story. You promised to be ready for me to-day, didn't you?" And Mr. Gray knit his brows, and looked angry and imperative.

"Yes, I promised. But——"

"Then keep your promise. No man has a right to break his word. Promises are sacred things, and should be kept religiously."

"If my customers had kept their promises to me, there would have been no failure in mine to you," answered the poor mechanic.

"It is of no use to plead other men's failings in justification of your own. You said the bill should be settled to-day; and I calculated upon it. Now, of all things in the world, I hate trifling. I shall not call again, sir!"

"If you were to call forty times, and I hadn't the money to settle your account, you would call in vain," said the mechanic, showing considerable disturbance of mind.

"You needn't add insult to wrong." Mr. Gray's countenance reddened, and he looked angry.

"If there is insult in the case, it is on your part; not mine," retorted the mechanic, with more feeling. "I am not a digger of gold out of the earth, nor a coiner of money. I must be paid for my work before I can pay the bills I owe. It was not enough that I told you of the failure of my customers to meet their engagements——"

"You've no business to have such customers—" broke in Mr. Gray—"No right to take my goods and sell them to men who are not honest enough to pay their bills."

"One of them is your own son," replied the mechanic, goaded beyond endurance. "His bill is equal to half of yours. I have sent for the amount a great many times, but still he puts me off with excuses. I will send it to you, next time."

This was thrusting home with a sharp sword, and the vanquished Mr. Gray retreated from the dattle field, bearing a painful wound."

"That wasn't right in me, I know," said the mechanic, as Gray left his shop. "I'm sorry, now, that I said it. But he pressed me too closely. I am but human."

"He is a hard, exacting, money-loving man," was my remark.

"They tell me he has become a Christian," said the mechanic. "Has got religion—been converted. Is that so?"

"It is common report; but I think common report must be in error. St. Paul gives patience, forbearance, long-suffering, meekness, brotherly kindness, and charity, as some of the Christian graces. I do not see them in this man. Therefore, common report must be in error."

"I have paid him a good many hundreds of dollars, since I opened my shop here," said the mechanic, with the manner of one who felt hurt. "If I am a poor, hard-working man, I try to be honest. Sometimes I get a little behind hand, as I am now, because people I work for don't pay up as they should. It happened twice before when I wasn't just square with Mr. Gray, and he pressed down very hard upon me, and talked just as you heard him to-day. He got his money, every dollar of it;

and he will get his money now. I did think, knowing that he had joined the church and made a profession of religion, that he would bear a little patiently with me, this time. That, as he had obtained forgiveness, as alleged, of his sins towards heaven, he would be merciful to his fellow-man. Ah, well! These things make us very sceptical about the honesty of men who call themselves religious. My experience with "professors," has not been very encouraging. As a general thing, I find them quite as greedy of gain as other men. We outside people of the world get to be very sharp-sighted. When a man sets himself up to be of better quality than we, and calls himself by a name significative of heavenly virtue, we judge him naturally, by his own standard, and watch him very closely. If he remain as hard, as selfish, as exacting, and as eager after money as before, we do not put much faith in his profession, and are very apt to class him with hypocrites. His praying, and fine talk about faith, and heavenly love, and being washed from all sin, excite in us contempt rather than respect. We ask for good works, and are never satisfied with anything else. By their fruits ye shall know them."

On the next Sunday I saw Mr. Gray in church. My eyes were on him when he entered. I noticed that all the lines of his face were drawn down, and that the whole aspect and bearing of the man were solemn and devotional. He moved to his place with a slow step, his eyes cast to the floor. On taking his seat, he leaned his head on the pew in front of him, and continued for nearly a minute in prayer. During the services I heard his voice in the singing; and through the sermon, he maintained the most fixed attention. It was communion Sabbath; and he remained, after the congregation was dismissed, to join in the holiest act of worship.

"Can this man be indeed self-deceived?" I asked myself, as I walked homeward. "Can he really believe that heaven is to be gained by pious acts alone. That every Sabbath evening he can pitch his tent a day's march nearer heaven, though all the week he have failed in the commonest offices of neighborly love?"

It so happened, that I had many opportunities for observing Mr. Gray, who, after joining the church, became an active worker in some of the public and prominent charities of the day. He contributed liberally in many cases, and gave a good deal of time to the prosecution of benevolent enterprises, in which men of some position were concerned. But, when I saw him dispute with a poor gardener who had laid sods in his yard, about fifty cents; take sixpence off of a weary strawberry woman; or chaffer with his bootblack over an extra shilling, I could not think that it was genuine love for his fellow men that prompted his ostentatious charities.

In no instance did I find any better estimation of him in business circles; for his religion did not chasten the ardor of his selfish love of advantage in trade; nor make him more generous, nor more inclined to help or befriend the weak and the needy. Twice I saw his action in the case of unhappy debtors, who had not been successful in business. In each case, his claim was among the smallest; but he said more unkind things, and was the hardest to satisfy, of any man among the creditors. He assumed dishonest intention at the outset, and made that a plea for the most rigid exactions; covering his own hard selfishness with offensive cant about mercantile honor, Christian integrity, and a religious observance of business contracts. He was the only man among all the creditors, who made his church-membership a prominent thing—few of them were even church-goers—and the only man who did not readily make concessions to the poor, down-trodden debtors.

"Is he a Christian?" I asked, as I walked home in some depression of spirits, from the last of these meetings. And I could but answer No—for, to be a Christian is to be Christ-like.

"As ye would that men should do to you, do ye even so to them." This is the divine standard. "Ye must be born again," leaves to us no latitude of interpretation. There must be a death of the old, natural, selfish loves, and a new birth of spiritual affections. As a man feels, so will he act. If the affections that rule in his heart be divine affections, he will be a lover of others, and a seeker of their good. He will not be a hard, harsh, exacting man in natural things, but kind, forbearing, thoughtful of others, and yielding. In all his dealings with men, his actions will be governed by the heavenly laws of justice and judgment. He will regard the good of his neighbor equally with his own. It is in the world where Christian graces reveal themselves, if they exist at all. Religion is not a mere Sunday affair, but the regulator of a man's conduct among his fellow-men. Unless it does this, it is a false religion, and he who depends upon it for the enjoyment of heavenly felicities in the next life, will find himself in miserable error. Heaven can not be earned by mere acts of piety, for heaven is the complement of all divine affections in the human soul; and a man must come into these—must be born into them—while on earth, or he can never find an eternal home among the angels of God. Heaven is not gained by doing, but by living.

VI.

OF SUCH IS THE KINGDOM OF HEAVEN.

"He is a very sick child," said the doctor, in answer to the mother's eager inquiries.

"Do you think him in danger?" The mother's face grew white, and her lips quivered.

The doctor, instead of replying to this question, gave some minute directions about the administration of certain medicines, and then turned from the luxurious bed upon which the child lay.

"How soon will you come again?" The mother, in her anxiety, caught hold of the doctor's arm, and held him fast.

"In the course of three or four hours. By that time the action of the medicine will be fully apparent. Give it punctually, and according to directions."

"Can't you remain?" urged the distressed mother, whose fears the doctor's unsatisfactory manner had aroused to the highest degree. "Oh, stay with him! There may be changes in an hour that your eyes should see. His life is in your hands, doctor; his precious life! Do not leave us!"

"Not in my hands, but in the hands of Him who holds the issues of life," replied the doctor. "We are but the instruments of healing."

"A little longer, doctor! stay a little longer!" urged the mother, scarcely rising a single degree in her perceptions above that first blind confidence in the physician's skill. But the doctor said:—

"That is impossible. Duty calls me to other bedsides. There is, but a short distance from here, a poor woman's only child as sick as yours, and as imperatively requiring my utmost skill. I must see it with as little delay as possible."

A poor woman's child! The mother turned half offended from the physician, and as he withdrew, sat down on the bed on which her sick boy lay, and taking one of his hot hands covered it with tears and kisses.

A poor woman's child! A washerwoman's, perhaps; or the common, coarse offspring of a mere sempstress; or of a German or Irish woman, living in a garret, amid dirt and disorder! And, for one such, her physician could leave the pure, sweet infant that lay suffering before her, of more value in her eyes than a thousand poor women's children.

"I couldn't have believed it of him!" sobbed the mother, in her selfishness and fear.

From the merchant's luxurious palace, into which disease had stolen on invisible wings, and stricken down the hope and pride of the house, the physician passed, and, in a few minutes, entered one of the meanest-looking houses in the neighborhood. The rich mother had not been far wrong in her conjecture. This visit was to a washerwoman's child. Up two naked, sand-covered pairs of stairs the doctor went, and pausing at a door in the third story, rapped lightly, and then, without waiting for the door to be opened, lifted the latch, and went in.

"Oh, doctor! I'm so glad you have come!" A pale, anxious-looking woman, with soiled and rumpled garments, and uncombed hair, sat holding a child in her arms. All of the preceding night, she had held him upon her lap, for he was too ill to sleep, and cried whenever she laid him upon the bed.

'How is he this morning?" inquired the doctor, as he sat down by the poor woman, and looked closely at the sick babe.

"Not any better. He's had a very bad night."

The doctor felt his pulse, examined his skin, noted the character of his respiration, and asked of the mother various questions relating to symptoms—all with a carefulness and interest as marked as he had shown at the visit just paid to the child of wealth and luxury. And quite as eagerly did this poor mother watch his countenance, and hang upon his few, unsatisfactory words, as did the mother from whom he had parted a little while before. To her heart, her babe was equally precious. Born though it was in poverty, and nurtured in toil, its presence was like sunlight in her humble dwelling, and its cooing voice the music that cheered her labor, and made her half forget the sadness of her recent widowhood.

"Do you think he will die, doctor?"

"While there is life there is hope," said the doctor, evading, with this old phrase, a direct answer.

"He is very sick?" The tearful mother still urged for some expression of opinion.

"He is a sick child. But, we will try the virtue of medicine, and trust in the Great Physician."

"Won't you come again to-day?" A harder heart than the doctor's could not have resisted that pleading look and tone.

"Yes; I will be round again in a few hours. In the meantime, give this medicine according to direction."

Three hours later, the doctor entered the palace-home of the rich mother. There was a troubled look on the face of the servant who admitted him; but he asked no questions. At the door of the sick chamber he paused a few moments, and listened; all within was still as death. Then he entered, but so softly, that none seemed to be aware of his presence. Around the bed on which the child lay stood a group of four or five persons, among them a clergyman, who had been sent for in haste, to comfort with words of heavenly import the heart of the mother, about to suffer its greatest earthly sorrow.

On the babe's ashen face the death-seal was so clearly impressed, that no eyes could be mistaken in the sign. Hope was extinguished even in the mother's heart.

How still it was in that luxurious chamber! Respiration was half suspended. In the presence of the dying babe, all felt a pervading consciousness of a divine presence. It seemed as if angels were about the child, waiting to bear upwards its pure spirit, just struggling to free itself from mortal investure. All but the mother stood up reverently, yet bending with earnest looks towards the beautiful babe—beautiful still, even though blighted with sickness,—but she sat cowering down at the bedside, her arm crushing the pillow on which the child lay, and her white face so full of anguish, that all eyes that looked upon it grew wet with tears.

Silently the doctor glided in, and made one of the waiting group. The babe's sight was veiled—the snowy lids having closed over the blue orbs that danced in light and beauty a few days before. The mouth, which pain had disfigured, was gradually recovering its sweet expression; and even while the change was passing, the image of a smile left thereon its soft imprint.

So gradual was the transition—so merciful was

the angel of death in his work of separating from mortal bonds the immortal spirit—that none who gazed on the infant knew the precise moment when the heart ceased to beat, and the lungs to respire.

First to move, in that statue-like group, was the clergyman. He was standing close beside the mother, whose blinding tears hid from her the true aspect of her babe's face. Bending towards her, he said, in a voice low, penetrating, and full of spiritual comfort,

"For of such is the kingdom of heaven!"

His words broke the spell. A wild cry from the mother's lips rent the air, and quivering sobs filled the apartment.

Ended, here, was the physician's work, and so, going noiselessly out, he departed, leaving the mourners in their sorrow, and with their dead. His duties were to the living.

His next visit was to the washerwoman's child. As he opened the door of the humble room he had left a few hours before, he saw the poor mother sitting, as he had last seen her, holding in her arms her sick babe. It needed no second glance to tell him that here, too, the physician's work was done.

There was no hope in the mother's tearless face; and no hope on the death-like countenance of the little sufferer.

Thus alone sat the mother with her dying babe on her lap. There were no friends to condole, no minister of religion to comfort. And yet, in the heart of the rich mother, whose child had just taken its everlasting departure, no purer love found abiding place; and no sadder grief came with its almost hopeless desolation of spirit, as the babe's eyes closed, and the lips, whose smile of beauty made the heart's daily sunshine, grew rigid in death.

"It is too late, doctor!" she said, looking up with a stony aspect, and speaking in a voice so calm and cold, that it almost chilled the physician's heart. "He is dying."

The doctor's work was not all done here. As a physician, his skill was of no further avail; but humanity had claims upon him. So he waited the issue of the struggle between life and death. It was brief, but not violent. The ministration was quite as merciful as in the former case. Very gently the spirit passed. There were no convulsions; no struggles; no evidences of pain; and the room seemed equally pervaded by angelic presence.

At last it was over, and the mother's face now covered with the first outflowing tears that had found vent for hours, was laid, in sorrow that no words could express, down against the cold face of her child.

"Of such is the kingdom of heaven!"

Not formally, nor of previous thought, were the words said. They fell from the doctor's lips almost spontaneously, and in tones as reverent and full of meaning as those in which he had heard the same words spoken a little while before. And they were just as true, in every shade of meaning in this case as in the other. Just as precious was this babe in the sight of heaven; just as lovingly was it received by angels; just as beautiful now is its celestial home; just as happy is it on the flowery slopes, and amid the green, sweet places of the garden of God.

"Of such is the kingdom of heaven!" Yes, of such. Of the pure and the innocent. Of the child-like in spirit. Of those who pass upwards in the innocence of ignorance, as little children; or, in the innocence of wisdom, as right-living men and women. It matters not for the external condition in either case. Only of *such*—the innocent and pure in spirit—is the kingdom of heaven, and they are to be found alike in the palace and in the cottage—among the rich and among the poor; for man is not regarded in heaven as to his externals, but as to his internals.

VII.

THE HAPPY NEW YEAR.

"Happy New Year, papa!" The sitting-room doors were thrown open, and a sweet little girl came bounding in. Her cheeks were all a-glow—smiles played around her cherry lips—her eyes were dancing with sunny light.

"Happy New Year, dear Papa!" And the next moment she was in her father's lap—her small arms clinging around his neck, and her rosy mouth pressed to his.

"Happy New Year, my sweet one!" responded Mr. Edgar, as he clasped the child fondly to his heart. "May all your New Years be happy," he added, in a low voice, and with a prayer in his heart.

Little Ellen laid her head in confiding love, against her father's breast, and he bent down his manly cheek until it rested on the soft masses of her golden hair.

To her it was a happy New Year's morning, and the words that fell from her lips were heart echoes. But it was not so to Mr. Edgar. The cares of this world, and the deceitfulness of riches, had, like evil weeds, found a rank growth in his spirit; while good seeds of truth, which, in earlier life, had sent forth their fresh green blades that lifted themselves in the bright, invigorating sunshine, gave now but feeble promise for the harvest time.

No, Mr. Edgar was not happy. There was a pressure on his feelings; an unsatisfied reaching out into the future; a vague consciousness of approaching evil. Very tenderly he loved his little one; and as she lay nestling against him, he could not help thinking of the time when he was a child, and when the New Years were happy ones. Ellen loved no place so well as her father's arms. When they were folded tightly around her, she had nothing more to desire; so she lay very still and silent, while the thoughts of her father wandered away from the loving child on his bosom to his own unsatisfied state of mind.

"For years," he said within himself, "I have been in earnest pursuit of the means of happiness, yet happiness itself seems every year to be still farther in the distance. There is something wrong. I cannot be in the true path. My days are busy and restless, my nights burdened with schemes that rarely do more than cheat my glowing fancy. What is the meaning of this?"

And Mr. Edgar fell into a deep revery, from which he was aroused by the voice of his wife, as she laid her hand upon his shoulder.

"A happy New Year, and many joyful returns!" she said in loving tones, as she pressed her lips to his forehead.

He did not answer. The tenderly spoken good wishes of his wife fell very gratefully, like refreshing dew upon his heart; but he was distinctly conscious of not being happy.

So far as worldly condition was concerned, Mr Edgar had no cause of mental depression. His business was prosperous under a careful management, and every year he saw himself better off by a few thousands of dollars. Always, however, it must be told, the number fell short of his expectations.

"There is something wrong." Mr. Edgar's thoughts were all running in one direction. A startling truth seemed suddenly to have been revealed to him, and he felt inclined to look at it in all possible aspects. "Why am I not happy?" That was urging the question home. But the answer was not given.

After breakfast, Mr. Edgar left home and went to his store. As he passed along the street, he saw at a window the face of a most lovely child. Her beauty, that had in it something of heavenly innocence, impressed him so deeply, that he turned to gain a second look, and in doing so, his eyes saw on the door of the dwelling the name of Abraham James. There was an instant revulsion of feeling; and for the first time that morning, Mr. Edgar remembered one of the causes of his uncomfortable state of mind. Abraham James was an unfortunate debtor who had failed to meet his obligations, among which were two notes of five hundred dollars each, given to Mr. Edgar. These had been placed by the latter in the hands of his lawyer, with directions to sue them out, and obtain the most that could be realized. Only the day before—the last day of the year—he had learned that there were two judgments that would take precedence of his, and sweep off a share of the debtor's property. The fact had chafed him considerably, causing him to indulge in harsh language towards his debtor. This language was not just, as he knew in his heart. But the loss of his money fretted him, and filled him with unkind feelings towards the individual who had occasioned the loss.

No wonder that Mr. Edgar was unhappy. As he continued on his way, the angry impulse that quickened the blood in his veins, subsided, and through the mist that obscured his mental vision, he saw the bright face of a child, the child of his unfortunate debtor. His own precious one was no lovelier—no purer; nor had her lips uttered on that morning in sweeter tones, the words—"A happy New Year, papa!"

How the thought thrilled him!

With his face bowed, and his eyes upon the ground, Mr. Edgar walked on. He could not sweep aside the image of that child at the window; nor keep back his thoughts from entering the dwelling where her presence might be the only sunbeam that gave light in its gloomy chambers.

"A happy New Year, papa!" Mr. Edgar almost started, for the words had so distinct an utterance to his inward ear, that they seemed as if spoken in the ambient air. In fancy, he had seen the troubled debtor, over whom hung many suits, his own among the rest, leaving the chamber where he had passed an almost sleepless night, and coming with slow steps and sad face to the family sitting-room. There, alone, with his face bowed upon his breast in gloomy reverie, Mr. Edgar had seen him; and while his heart was enlarged with pity and sympathy, the door opened—light footsteps moved across the room —a child sprang into his arms, and a glad voice exclaimed—

"A happy New Year, papa!"

When Mr. Edgar arrived at his store, his feelings towards Mr. James were very different from what they were on the day previous. All anger—all resentment—were gone, and kindness had taken their place. What if Mr. James did owe him a thousand dollars? What if he should lose the whole amount of this indebtedness? Was the condition of the former so much better than his own, that he would care to change places with him? The very idea caused a shudder to run along his nerves.

"Poor man!" he said to himself, pityingly.

"What a terrible thing to be thus involved in debt—thus crippled, thus driven to the wall. It would kill me! Men are very cruel to each other, and I am cruel with the rest. What are a thousend dollars to me, or a thousand dollars to my well-to-do neighbor, compared with the ruin of a helpless fellow-man! James asked time; in two years he was sure he could recover himself and make all good. But, with a heartlessness that causes my cheek to burn as I think of it, I answered—'The first loss is always the best loss. I will get what I can, and let the balance go.' The look he then gave me, has troubled my conscience ever since. No wonder it is not a happy New Year."

Scarcely had Mr. Edgar passed the dwelling of his unfortunate creditor, when the latter, who had been walking the floor of his parlor in a troubled state of mind, came to the window and stood by his child, who was dear to him as a child could be to the heart of a father.

"Happy New Year, papa!" It was the third time since morning dawn that he had received this greeting from the same sweet lips—the third time that her kisses were given with the heart-warmth of childhood's unselfish love.

Mr. James tried to give back the same glad greeting, but the words seemed to choke him, and failed in the utterance. As the two stood by the window, the wife and mother came up, and leaning against her husband, looked forth with a sad heart. Oh no! it was not a happy new year's morning to them. Long before the dawn of another year, they must go forth from their pleasant home; and both their hearts shrunk back in fear from the dark beyond.

"Good morning, dear," said Mr. James, soon afterwards, as, with hat, and coat, and muffler on, he stood ready to go forth to meet the business trials of the day. His voice was depressed, and his countenance sad. Mrs. James did not say "Good morning," in turn. But her husband saw the motion of her lips and the tears in her eyes, and he knew what was in her heart.

The business assigned to that day was a painful one for Mr. James. The only creditor who had commenced a suit was Mr. Edgar, he having declined entering into any arrangement with the other creditors, coldly saying that, in his opinion, "the first loss was always the best loss," and that extensions were, in most cases, equivalent to the abandonment of a claim. He was willing to take what the law would give him. Pursuant to this view, a suit had been brought, and the debtor, to anticipate the result, confessed judgment to two of his largest creditors, who honorably bound themselves to see that a *pro rata* division was made of all his effects.

The business of this New Year's Day, was to draw up as complete a statement as possible of his affairs, and Mr. James went about the work with a heavy heart. He had been engaged in this way for over an hour, when one of his clerks came to the desk where he was writing, and handed him a letter which a lad had just brought in. He broke the seal with a nervous foreboding of trouble, for, of late, these letters by the hands of the private messengers, had been frequent, and rarely of an agreeable character. From the envelope, as he commenced withdrawing the letter, there dropped upon the desk a narrow piece of paper, folded like a bill. He took it up with almost reluctant fingers, and slowly pressed back the ends so as to read its face, and comprehend its import.

Twice his eyes went over the brief lines, before he was clear as to their meaning. They were as follows:

"Received, January 1, 18—, of Abraham James, One Thousand Dollars, in full of all demands.

"HIRAM EDGAR."

Hurriedly, now, did Mr. James unfold the letter that accompanied this receipt. Its language moved him deeply:

"ABRAHAM JAMES, Esq.,

DEAR SIR: I was not in a right state of mind when I gave directions to have a suit brought against you. I have seen clearer since, and wish to act from a better principle. My own affairs are prosperous. During the year which has just closed, my profits have been better than in any year since I started business. Your affairs, on the contrary are unprosperous. Heavy losses, instead of fair profits, are the result of a year's tireless efforts, and you find yourself near the bottom of the wheel, while I am sweeping upwards. As I think of this, and of my unfeeling conduct towards you in your misfortunes, I am mortified as well as pained. There is an element in my character which ought not to be there. I am self-convicted of cruelty. Accept, my dear sir, in the enclosed receipt, the best reparation in my power to make. In giving up this claim, I do not abandon an item that goes to complete the sum of my happiness. Not a single comfort will be abridged. It will not shrink the dimensions of my house, nor withdraw from myself or family any portion of food or raiment. Accept, then, the New Year's gift I offer, and believe that I have a purer delight in giving than you in receiving. My best wishes are with you for the future, and if, in anything, I can aid you in your arrangements with creditors, do not fail to command my service.

"Most truly yours,

"HIRAM EDGAR.'

For the space of nearly five minutes, Mr. James sat very still, the letter of Mr. Edgar before him. Then he folded it up, with the receipt inside, and placed it in his pocket; then he put away the inventories he had been examining, and tore up several pieces of paper, on which were sundry calculations; and then he put on his warm overcoat and buttoned it to the chin.

"Edward," said Mr. James, as he walked down the store, "I shall not return this afternoon. It is New Year's Day, and you can close up at two o'clock."

It cost Mr. Edgar a struggle to write the receipt in full. A thousand dollars was a large sum of money to give away by a single stroke of the pen. Love of gain and selfishness pleaded strongly for the last farthing; but the better reason and better feelings of the man prevailed, and the good deed was done. How light his heart felt—how suddenly the clouds were lifted from his sky, and the strange pressure from his feelings! It was to him a new experience.

On the evening that closed the day—the first evening of the New Year—Mr. Edgar sat with his wife and children in his elegant home, happier by far than he was in the morning, and almost wondering at the change in his state of mind. Little Ellen was in his arms, and as he looked upon her cherub face, he thought of a face as beautiful, seen by him in the morning, at the window of his unfortunate debtor. The face of an angel it had proved to him, for it prompted the good deed from which had sprung a double blessing. While he sat thus, he heard the door bell ring. In a few minutes the waiter handed in a letter. He broke the seal and read:

"My Dear Sir:

"This morning my dear little Aggy, the light of our home, greeted me with a joyous 'Happy New Year.' I took her in my arms and kissed her, keeping my face close to hers, that she might not see the sadness of mine. Ah, sir! The day broke in gloom. The words of my child found no echo in my heart. I could have wept over her, if the strength of manhood had not risen above the weakness of nature. But all is changed now. A few minutes ago the 'Happy New Year' was flowing to me from the sweet lips of my child, and the words went thrilling in gladness to my heart. May the day close as happily for you and yours, as it is closing for me and mine.

"God bless you!

"Abraham James."

Mr. Edgar read this letter twice, and then handed it, without a word, to his wife.

"What is the meaning of this? I do not understand it, Hiram." Mrs. Edgar looked wonderingly into her husband's face.

The story, to which she listened eagerly, was briefly told. When Mr. Edgar had finished, his wife arose, and, with tears of love and sympathy in her eyes, crossed over to where he was sitting, and throwing her arms around his neck, said:

"My good, my generous husband! I feel very proud of you this night. That was a noble deed; and I thank you for it in the name of our common humanity."

Never had words from the lips of his wife sounded so pleasantly in the ears of Mr. Edgar. Never had he known so happy a New Year's Day as the one which had just closed; and, though it saw him poorer than he believed himself in the morning, by nearly a thousand dollars, he was richer in feeling—richer in the heart's unwasting possessions—than he had ever been in his life.

VIII.

ENTERING HEAVEN.

"The gates of heaven have swung open, and another soul has entered its shining courts," said the preacher, as he stood, with uncovered head, by the coffin of one whose mortal history was closed.

As I left the grave-yard, an old man, of mild aspect, walked by my side.

"Did you know Mr. ——?" he asked, referring to the deceased.

"As a neighbor, but not intimately," was my reply.

"I knew him very well," said one who walked with us.

"The preacher spoke of him as having entered heaven," the old man quietly remarked.

"He died calmly and in Christian hope, putting his trust in his Redeemer," said the other "I was with him in his last moments, and his end was peace. If he has not gone to heaven, there are not many of us who can look forward with confidence."

"We must enter heaven while living upon the earth," said the old man, in answer to this, speaking gravely, "or the doors will be for ever shut against us. We must be, as to our spirits, in the society of angels here, or we cannot be in association with them hereafter."

"How can we be in heaven and upon earth at the same time?" queried the one who had spoken of my neighbor's peaceful end; "for one is spiritual and the other natural."

"To be spiritual-minded is to be in heaven; and this we may be, while, as to the natural body, we are still upon the earth. Was our friend spiritual-minded?"

The old man turned to our companion, and awaited his answer.

"He did not talk much of religion, as a general thing; but he was a regular church-goer."

"That signifies little," was replied.

"He was as good as other men; better in many things, I should think—though not in any way distinguished for piety. He was not one of your talking professors. But those who knew him best, valued him most. His peaceful end assures me that he is safe."

"The life, not the death, gives genuine assurance," said the old man. "With rare exceptions, all men die peacefully—the evil and the good. As the time of departure draws near, the soul sinks into tranquil states, and thoughts of life, not death, hold it away from depressing influences. There is a wise as well as a merciful providence in this. But, you say, that those who knew him best, valued him most."

"Yes."

"Valued him for what?"

"For his kindness of heart, his benevolence, his truth and honesty. Why, sir, that man would have suffered his right arm to be taken, rather than swervo from his integrity."

"Was he proud of his honest fame? Did he boast of it, and compare himself with other men?"

"No, sir. He was not one who thought much of himself, or took merit for a good deed. I think the poor will miss him, and weak ones sigh for the sustaining hand that is now cold in death. Ah, sir, he was a good man. But I don't think he could be called spiritual-minded."

"A good man, and a true man, and yet not spiritual-minded!" There was a look of surprise in the old man's face. "Are not goodness and truth spiritual in their nature? And does not their reception into any mind determine its quality?"

"You may be right in your conclusions," said the other. "I have not been in the habit of viewing things just in your way. But I am very sure that our friend has gone to heaven."

"He has gone among those who are like him, and with whom he was in conjunction as to his spirit, while he yet lived in the world," the old man answered. "He could not live in eternal association with spirits or angels, the movement of whose lives was not in harmony with his own. If he was a lover of truth; if he was kind, benevolent, thoughtful of others, and faithful in all his acts, he has passed upwards into the heavenly companionship of the good; but if he was selfish, cruel, exacting, and faithless in his life, no tranquil death-hour has made him a fit companion for angels, and he will go unto his own. Revelation affirms this, and reason assents to no other conclusion. It is a doctrine that sweeps away fallacious hopes, and leaves to none the dangerous, if not always fatal, experiment of a death-bed repentance."

We paused, for our ways diverged.

"If all were of your doctrine," said I, "men would take more heed to their ways. There are few who do not hope to reach heaven at last. They trust to some good deed that will not involve any hard denial of self, or to some cheap act of faith, to crowd them through the gate, thinking that if they once get in, they will be all right for eternity. But this idea of a heavenly quality being formed in the soul before any one can enter heaven, is rather a hard saying for most men. It is an extinguisher of hope for the evil-minded."

"There is no other way," was answered. "We must enter through the strait gate of self-denial—and it will be found very strait to most people. If we fail to do this, and seek to climb up some other way, the consequences of our folly will be with us for ever."

And as the old man said this, we turned from him, pondering his words in our hearts.

IX.

IT IS MORNING WITH THE CHILD.

A MOTHER sat, in tears, by the bed-side of her youngest-born, and best beloved. Six days had passed since the hand of fever was laid upon him, and, ever since, the life-fountains had been drying up under the fervent heat. Many times daily had she entered into her closet and bowed herself before the Father of Mercies, praying that the Destroyer might pass by her dwelling. But prayers and tears availed not. Steadily the disease kept on its fatal course, and now scarcely a hope remained. Friends gathered around, offering words of consolation, but they were only as idle murmurs in her ears.

"The Lord giveth and the Lord taketh away—Blessed be the name of the Lord," said the good pastor, who, only a year before, had lifted the sweet boy in his arms, and, in the presence of angels, touched his pure forehead with the waters of baptism.

But the mother made no sign. She could not accept this affliction as a blessing—she could not offer up thanks. Her very life was bound up in the life of her child, and the thought of separation was so terrible that no place for consolation was left in her grieving spirit.

"It is appointed unto man once to die," added the minister, still seeking to penetrate the mother's heart, and pour in oil and wine; "we must all pass by this way—must all enter this valley—must all go down into the dark river. How much better, then, to die in the morning of life, ere fierce sunbeams have drank the fragrant dews, or the green leaves have withered on the sapless branches."

Still the mother made no sign.

"You will have a treasure in heaven; and where the treasure is, there will the heart be also."

But all availed not. The tears fell like rain.

Sadly, at length, the minister turned away, and left the weeping mother with her friends; for her ears were closed to all the words of consolation he could offer.

An hour later, and the mother still bent over the

frail body of her little one. There was no hope in her heart, for she saw upon his wan face the signet mark of the death-angel. One friend remained with her; and, until now, this friend had offered no words of comfort. The grieving mother was bending over the pillow upon which the sick child lay, and gazing down upon the countenance she was soon to see no more, when she felt a hand laid gently upon her own, and with a touch that sent a new impulse throbbing through the heart.

"It is very dark here, sometimes," said the friend, very softly, very tenderly, and with a meaning in her voice beyond that contained in the words she had uttered.

The mother answered only by a returning pressure of the hand.

"Even the light of this world is darkness when compared with the light of heaven. Here the best and most highly favored do little more than grope their way. There, every one walks in noon-day clearness."

She had gained the mother's ear. Her words had gone inward to the region of thought.

"I have passed through these deep waters, my friend," she continued, "and have heard their terrible roaring. I have held a dying babe in my arms, and clung to it with an agony of grief that seemed as if it would snap my very heart-strings. But, after the keenness of affliction was over, I had this consolation, and it has remained ever since. When the night with *me* was at the darkest, it was morning with *my child.* Yes, it was then that the morning broke on him which shall never go down in night. Blessed morning of celestial glory! Oh, how often and often since, when I have walked in darkness, have I thanked God, with a true heart, fervently, that it was morning with my child!"

The mother's tears ceased to fall, and she turned her wet eyes upon her friend, and looked into her face earnestly.

"There is one question," said the friend, after a pause, "that every mother should ask herself. It is this—'How do I love my child—selfishly or unselfishly?' If unselfishly, then, whatever is best for the child, will give to her heart the deepest pleasure. I had a dream on the very night my precious one was taken away from me. I believe that it was imaged to my fancy while sleeping, by a loving angel sent to comfort me in my great affliction. There had always been something very fearful to me in the idea of dying here, and awakening to consciousness in a new and strangely different existence; and the thought followed my child. That dream was to me a revelation, and as such I accepted it thankfully. I saw, in my sleep, two scenes—the one contrasting with the other, as we sometimes see them in pictures. One scene represented the saddest of my life-experiences. I saw myself sitting in darkness and in tears, as you sit now, my friend and sister, bending over my precious babe, clinging to it as the miser clings to his gold—aye, and with an intenser passion. But only a veil dropped down between that scene and another, which quickly enchained my vision, and caused my heart, heavy with grief, to throb with a new-born pleasure. An angel, in form like a chaste young virgin, was clasping to her bosom a babe, in all the ecstasy of a new-born joy. No mother, when she feels upon her breast the first pressure of her first babe, ever felt more delight than I saw pictured in the face of the angel as she held *my* babe to her loving heart. Yes, *my* babe, just born into heaven, and given into her care by the Divine Father of us all.

"For a time I could not withdraw my eyes

from the face of the angel. Never had I gazed upon a countenance so full of love; so radiant with celestial beauty. And the babe nestled on her bosom as lovingly as it had ever nestled on mine. From this scene, after gazing upon it until tears ran down my cheeks—tears of gratitude that it was so well with my babe—I turned to look at the darker one—at the sorrowing earthly mother and the suffering child! Poor babe! Wasted with sickness and writhing with mortal pain. How yearningly and pityingly my heart went towards it, and I prayed for its deliverance! Even as the words went up from my heart, the darker scene faded until it became no longer visible; but the brighter one remained. When I awoke, and grief for my great loss revived in my heart, I recalled the precious dream, and took comfort. What if I did walk in darkness? It was morning—eternal morning, with my child!"

As the mother listened, to her mind was also pictured the two scenes. Her tears had ceased to flow, and her countenance showed a visible interest. A little while she sat musing, and then, as she turned her eyes, full of tenderness, upon her sick boy, said:

"Oh, it is hard, very hard, to give him up!—How can I do it? How can I resign him, even to the care of an angel?"

The friend said no more. Her words had found a way into the heart of the sorrowing one, and she left them to do their own work.

A little later, and the hour of deepest darkness came—the hour of separation. Over the mother's spirit a pall of blackest gloom was spread. The words of her friend had faded from her memory. She saw not the beautiful beyond, but gazed only upon a dark, gloomy abyss, into which her precious one was about falling, while she stood helpless by. Oh, what would she not then have given for light upon the future!—for an unsealed vision. Willingly would she have died, that she might go with her child along the unknown way, and shield him from its terrors. Over him she bent, seeing nothing, hearing nothing, caring for nothing but her boy; while darker and closer the shadows gathered around her. It was night—dark, cold, moonless night, with the grieving mother.

For more than an hour the child had lain in a deep stupor, but it was evident that life was ebbing away, and that the last agony would soon be over. For herself, the mother had almost ceased to grieve: every thought and every feeling were centered in her child, about passing alone through the gate of death—alone to meet the realities of the unseen world.

Suddenly a light fell upon the wan, suffering face—a smile played around the white lips—the eyes, long closed, and heavy with pain and fever, flew open, and, glancing upwards with a glad expression, the child said,

"Good morning, mamma!"

"Good morning, love!" answered the startled mother, scarcely thinking of the words she uttered.

"Good morning!" repeated the child, still gazing upwards, with a new and heavenly beauty in its countenance. "Oh, it is morning now!"

Fixed was the glad look for several moments; then the fringing lids drooped slowly, until they lay softly upon the pure white cheeks. The parted lips closed; but the smile remained. The hands, lifted for a moment in glad surprise, fell over the placid breast, and all was still, and holy, and beautiful.

"Yes, it is morning now," whispered the friend in the mother's ear, as she sat like one entranced, gazing upon the pulseless form before her, which, as if touched by an enchanter's wand, had suddenly changed from an image of suffering into one of tranquil beauty.

And it *was* morning with the child—a heavenly morning—and morning also with the mother; for a new light had dawned upon her, and a new faith in the hereafter. The dark valley was suddenly bridged with light, and she saw her precious one by angel guides led safely over.

"God careth for these jewels," said the friend, a few hours afterwards. "They are precious in his sight: not one of them is lost. His love is tenderer even than a mother's love. We may trust them in his hands with unfaltering confidence. Yes, yes, grieving mother! it is indeed morning with your babe!"

X.

RICHER, OR POORER?

It was the last day and last evening of the week and of the year; and Mr. Stephens sat alone, reviewing the incidents of his life during the twelve months now just completed.

"I think," he said within himself, "that I have cause of self-congratulation. Providence has specially favored me. All my work has prospered."

Yet, even while he thus referred to a providential agency, the pride of human prudence was swelling in his heart.

"How many a goodly vessel has been shattered to pieces on the seething breakers; yet my staunch ship still rides the waves in safety."

Mr. Stephens arose from his chair, as he said this, and drawing his thumbs into the arm holes of his waistcoat, threw his head back and his chest forward, and commenced pacing the floor of his elegant parlor with the air of a man who felt at peace with himself and all the world. As he walked, he said, half-aloud—

"Providence has smiled on me, and I am thankful. God has crowned my seasons with blessing. To-morrow, on the first Sabbath of the new year, I will give him thanks in the congregation of his people; for the Lord accepteth a thankful heart. Many a man," he continued, "has lost his earthly good things, for lack of a thankful heart. Mine shall abound in gratitude."

And then Mr. Stephens, by a natural progression of thought, began making a hurried estimate of his gains for the year. They were large. As he resumed his seat in the great cushioned chair, he said, with a flutter of pleased emotions—

"I am richer to-day, by many thousands, than I was a year ago."

"Richer—yes richer"—he murmured, half aloud, as if speaking to some one. Several minutes had passed, and, with eyes partly closed, he was sinking down among the soft cushions of his chair. From waking consciousness to sleeping vision there is, sometimes, scarcely a moment's interval. It was so in the present case.

"Richer—richer," was still upon the merchant's lips, when the rustle of garments reached his ears, and he saw by his side a form of angelic beauty.

"And yet," said a voice that went thrilling to the very centre of his life, "you have lost fearfully."

"Lost! lost! Oh, no—I have lost nothing," answered the merchant, quickly recovering himself. "Every venture has proved successful."

"Let us see." And the strange visitor sat down just in front of Mr. Stephens, and fixed her calm, searching eyes upon his face. "If I have estimated correctly, you are vastly poorer now, than you were at the year's beginning."

"A low shudder of fear ran along the merchant's nerves. What could this mean? He thought of his solid real estate, his well-secured stocks, his bonds, his ships, and his merchandise.

"I am richer, not poorer,'" he answered with regaining confidence.

"You have lost integrity," said the visitor, "one of the priceless jewels of a man's life."

"I am an honest man." The merchant spoke with a flush of indignation upon his face.

"Honest before men—not before God. You

have forgotten that an All-seeing eye was upon you."

"What have I done? Bring my deeds to the light. I have wronged no man."

The merchant's voice was confident.

The visitor handed him, in silence, a narrow piece of paper, on which were some written and printed words.

"What is this?" he read, and answered his own question—"Oh, a tax bill." His tone was indifferent.

"Is it paid?"

"Paid! I have never seen it before."

"You believed yourself forgotten, in this particular instance, by assessor and collector," said the visitor severely, "and counted this sum as so much in the year's gain. You knew that the debt existed; that you owed the State just so much for the protection it gave to your life and property. That so much was due as an item in your contribution in support of order, education, and the helpless poor. But this high obligation you have willfully set aside, and indulged a feeling of selfish pleasure at the trifling gain it left in your hands—gain of less than a hundred perishable dollars!"

A cold chill of conviction struck to the heart of Mr. Stephens.

"But the loss is fearful to think of," was continued. "Loss of manly integrity and heavenly virtue. No one could know of this, you said within your heart. Or, if it were discovered that an assessment had been omitted, or a bill mislaid, it would only be regarded as an error, and your prompt settlement, on presentation, would put you all right in the world's regard. Ah, sir,—in the trial of your integrity, honor failed. In the hour of temptation, you fell. Is this gain, or loss? Are you richer, or poorer, by the act?

The merchant's head sank low upon his breast in shame and self-condemnation. It was all too true. He had, knowingly, omitted to pay a tax bill that was justly due. Had failed that much in one of his higher obligations to society, and for the paltry gain of a few dollars. In all his public walk before men, he had maintained an upright stature; but stooped to a petty fraud in secret.

"A fearful loss," said the visitor, "for it is a loss of just so much of the property that goes to make up a man's riches in heaven. I said you were poorer now than at this time last year; and so you are, by this large item. And you have lost, besides, a pearl of inestimable value; one that you could have taken with you as a rich inheritance into the other life. God gave you an opportunity to help a brother in need, who came to you in his sore distress, and tried to awaken your sympathy. But you heard him only in part, and turned him aside with cold and cutting words. It was not enough that you saw the struggles of manly pride in his face, and the pale anguish of features; not enough that he was weak and in sore trouble—you must add rebuke to denial, as if misfortune were a crime. As a merchant, you had prospered in every venture—you were at ease, and in comfort; and so God sent to you this man, that you might help him in his need, and thus add to your heavenly riches. But love of self triumphed over a love of the neighbor. You preferred gold to good.—The treasures that moth and rust corrupt, to that which is enduring as eternity. The pure pearl of tender compassion was offered for your acceptance, but your eyes were too dim to see its priceless value. God did not forget his needy child. The good deed you failed to do, another performed, and to him heaven sent the blessing that might have been yours. And so there is more lost treasure to be taken into the account."

"Spare me!" cried the merchant, raising his hands with a deprecating gesture. "Oh, spare me!"

Not yet," said the visitor. "Money gave you power, and you used that power to wrong thousands of your weaker fellow-men."

"I have wronged no one," answered the merchant boldly. "All my dealings have been in justice between man and man."

"You deceive yourself, returned the visitor "Is mere speculation honest?" Is it just to monopolize an article that the poorest mechanic and humblest day-laborer must have, and so enhance its price that many comforts must be given up in order to procure the needed supply? You have not been just between man and man, for you have done this, and done it at the peril of your soul; for loss of neighborly regard and honest principle were involved in the act. Gold gained by fair trading did not come in fast enough to satisfy your thirst for riches, and so you laid plans, that were too successful, for defrauding your weaker brethren. You diminished the supply of bread in the mouths of hungry children, and made the poor man's burdens heavier, that you might add to the wealth already increased beyond your power to enjoy."

Again the head of Mr. Stephens sank upon his breast, and he was covered with shame and confusion.

"Is there cause for self-congratulation in this? Are you really a richer man to-night than you were at the year's beginning?"

"Leave me!" said the merchant, with a groan of anguish.

"Not yet; for my mission is incomplete," answered the beautiful monitor. "It is said that Mr. Stephens is a high-minded, honorable merchant. Every where, in business circles, men bear this testimony in his favor."

The merchant began recovering himself. A glow of pride warmed his heart.

"Men can can say nothing less," he made answer.

"Let your own heart judge. What better are you than the thief who appropriates unlawfully the goods of another? Or what honor is there in taking, by constraint, a dollar from the earnings of ten thousand different men, in order that you may add ten thousand dollars to your heaped-up store of wealth? This you have done in a single act of unrighteous speculation. What would you think of the morality of a newsboy who should, by some adroit piece of petty circumvention, succeed in extracting a sixpence from the pockets of each of a dozen ragged companions, that he might be possessor of the most money, or secure the means of enjoyment which poverty denied to them? You would consider him a sharper; perhaps, call him a rogue. Covetousness was the spring of action in your case, as it would be in his; and a selfish disregard of the neighbor led on to the consummation of wrong.

"High-minded and honorable!" There was an almost withering contempt in the monitor's voice. "If it would not be honorable in the newsboy to get, without any return of benefits, the sixpences of his humble companions, it cannot be honorable in the scheming merchant to wrong his neighbors on a broader scale. Take a thousand dollars of your money and place it here on this table—the money you gained in that nice speculation for which so many shrewd, unscrupulous men praised your boldness and sagacity. Count it over, coin by coin, and as you look upon each one successively, say thus to yourself: 'This dollar I took from a poor day-laborer. He had saved it, penny by penny; and as he saved, the hope of getting something ahead cheered him in his ill-requited work. But, my plans were too well laid; the dollar passed from its little treasury, and now is mine. The man grew discouraged at its loss, and went back to his dram-drinking. He lies in prison now, and his children are beggars on the street. That dollar cost something. This one has almost as sad a story: A toiling mother, with three helpless babes to support, was barely able to procure food and raiment, though she bent to her weary work long after midnight. I raised the price of bread, and this extra dollar she had to earn by increasing toil. And so count on, coin after coin, until you get the full sum of human suffering your base speculation in food has cost. Honorable! high-minded! No, sir! In the sight of Heaven you appear mean, base, selfish, and dishonorable."

Again the merchant's head was depressed, and his heart sunk like lead in his bosom. His own deformed image was before him, and he shuddered at the monstrous effigy.

"I do not think you are any richer for that scheme of wrong and oppression," resumed the visitor.

"If your soul were required of you this night, you could not take a dollar of gain with you; but instead, only the curse of an evil deed. Shall I go on?"

"No! no! in Heaven's name, spare me!" cried the merchant aloud, starting up and turning to fly from his rebuking visitor. But, even while he spoke, the beautiful being faded from his sight, and he found himself alone in his parlor. The vision had passed, but the lesson remained.

The next day was the first Sabbath of the new year. Mr. Stevens went to church, as he had purposed—not, however, to give thanks for a prosperous year, but to humble himself; to ask forgiveness of sin, and to pray for the inspiration of a better life. The minister preached from these searching words: "For what shall it profit a man, if he gain the whole world and lose his own soul; or what shall a man give in exchange for his soul?" And every word of the sermon seemed as if addressed to the conscience-stricken merchant. The unpaid tax-bill; the unrighteous speculation; the failure to help a brother in need, were all educed, and marked by special condemnation. The mirror was a second time held up, and Mr. Stevens looked once more, in shame, upon the marred image of himself.

"God helping me," he said devoutly, as he walked homeward, "I will be a richer man on the next new-year's day than I am on this—richer in heavenly possessions, the best of all."

And it was so.

XI.

EVERY WRINKLE A LINE OF BEAUTY.

"I DON'T like old people," said a thoughtless young girl, "they are either cross, disagreeable, or ugly."

"You have been unfortunate in your chances of observation," replied a lady, sitting near her.

"It may be so, but I speak, at least, from experience. All the old people it has been my fortune, or misfortune, to meet, have been cross in temper and repulsive in appearance. I have an old aunt who is always associated in my mind with the Witch of Endor. From a child I have had a perfect horror of her. I doubt if she ever gave utterance to a kind or uncomplaining word in her life."

"You must not judge all by this aunt, my young friend," said the lady. "There are handsome and agreeable old people in the world, and not a few of them either, but many. Age does not necessarily sour the temper, nor mar the countenance. There is such a thing as 'growing old gracefully,' and the number of those who are thus advancing along the paths of life, I am pleased to say, are increasing yearly. I happen to have an old aunt also, but, so far from being a second Witch of Endor, I heard a gentleman, not many days ago, remark, in speaking of her, 'Why, every wrinkle in Mrs. Elder's face is a line of beauty.' And so it is; for every wrinkle there was born of patient endurance, or unselfish devotion to the good of others. I look at her dear old face often and often, and say to myself, 'Now, is she not handsome?'"

"I should really like to see your aunt," said the young girl, half skeptically.

"Come to my house to-morrow, and we will pay her a visit," answered the lady. "It will do both of us good."

"Thank you for the invitation. I will certainly call."

The next day came, and the young lady was early at the house of Mrs. Barton.

"Glad to see you, Kate," was the pleasant greeting she received. "We are to call on my aunt Elder, I believe."

"Yes; you promised to introduce me to an old lady who, so far from being cross and ugly, is sweet-tempered and beautiful. The sweet temper I can imagine, but not a face wrinkled and beautiful at the same time."

"You shall see," was answered.

"Ah, good morning, Mary," said a low, but very pleasant and cheerful voice, as the two ladies entered the small but neat and orderly sitting-room of Mrs. Elder.

"My friend, Miss Kate Williams," said Mrs. Barton, presenting the young lady.

Mrs. Elder laid her knitting upon a table, close to her open Bible, and rising, took the hand of Miss Williams, looking earnestly into her young face as she did so, and smiling so sweet a welcome, that Kate did not see a wrinkle, for the beautiful light that shone from the old lady's placid countenance.

"I am always pleased to see young faces," said Mrs. Elder, "and to feel the warmth of young hearts."

"How are you to-day, aunt?" inquired Mrs. Barton.

"Not so well in body as when you were here last. I sleep but poorly."

Mrs. Elder smiled as if she were telling of enjoyments, and then added—

"But this is only one of the penalties of age. I knew it must come, and long ago made up my mind to be patient and enduring. These are some of the light afflictions, lasting but for a moment, which, if borne in Christian meekness, help to work out for us that far more exceeding and eternal weight of glory, to which the apostle refers in one of his sublime passages."

Miss Williams looked at the old lady half wonderingly.

"Always doing something, Aunt Elder," said Mrs. Barton, placing her hand upon the half-knit yarn stocking which the old lady had put aside as she rose to take the hand of Miss Williams. "Knitting, I suppose, has grown into a kind of habit. The act brings its own reward. It is your pleasant pastime."

"No, child, not my pleasant pastime, but my useful employment," answered Mrs. Elder. "I can't do much in this world for other people; still I can do a little, and I am thankful for the privilege; for I don't believe it is possible for anybody to be happy who is not engaged in some useful employment. I manage to keep the children of half a dozen poor families in warm stockings for the winter, and that is something added to the common stock of human comfort."

The eyes of Miss Williams were now fixed intently upon the old lady's age-marked features. Wrinkles went curving about her cheeks, her lips, and chin, and wrinkles planted themselves deeply upon her forehead. Grey hairs were visible beneath her cap-border; her calm eyes lay far back in their hollow sockets; the symmetry of her mouth was gone; and yet it seemed to the young girl, as she gazed at her wonderingly, as if every wrinkle in that aged face were indeed a line of beauty!

"But you must have a surer foundation for happiness than knitting stockings," said Mrs. Barton.

The old lady seemed thoughtful for a moment. She then said, with sweet impressiveness—

"There is only one foundation upon which we can rest and find happiness, and that is God's love in the heart. The great question for us all is, How to obtain that love. It will not come at our command. We cannot drag it down from heaven. We cannot find it, search we ever so diligently. God's love is God-given; and he bestows it only upon those who first have neighborly love. This is that higher love's receptacle in the human heart. First, love of the neighbor; then, love of good, which is divine love in the soul, the sure foundation for abiding happiness. So you see, Mary, the value of even knitting stockings to one like me. It is useful work, and that, as the old monk said, is worship."

Miss Williams could not withdraw her eyes from the old lady's face. Its beauty and its goodness seemed to fascinate her. She was a girl of quick feelings and some enthusiasm. Suddenly rising from the chair she had taken a few moments before, she came forward, and stooping over Mrs. Elder, kissed her, almost reverently, on the forehead, saying, as she did so—

"May I be like you when I grow old—every wrinkle in my face a line of beauty!"

"Grow old in goodness, my dear young friend!" answered Mrs. Elder, taking her hand tightly within her own, and speaking with emotion—for the young girl's sudden speech had stirred her feelings to an unusual depth—"Grow old in goodness, through the discipline of self-denial and the gentle leadings of neighborly love. It is the only path that conducts to a peaceful old age."

"Thanks for the lesson you have taught me," said Miss Williams, when she again clasped the hand of Mrs. Elder in parting. "I will try to grow old, as the years pass inevitably onwards, in the better way that you have walked. And may my last days be, like yours, my best days, and radiant with light shining down from the better world."

"I am a skeptic no longer" (she was now in the street with Mrs. Barton); "beauty and age are not incompatible."

"But the beauty of age," replied Mrs. Barton, "is unlike the beauty of youth; the one is natural, the other spiritual and celestial. The one is of the earth—earthly; the other is of the heavens—heavenly. An evil soul gradually mars the face, until every lineament becomes repulsive; but a soul of goodness continually recreates the countenance, and covers it with living beauty."

XII.

DIED POOR.

"It was a sad funeral to me," said the speaker; "the saddest I have attended for many years."

"That of Edmonson?"

"Yes."

"How did he die?"

"Poor—poor as poverty. His life was one long struggle with the world, and at every disadvantage. Fortune mocked him all the while with golden promises that were destined never to know fulfillment."

"Yet, he was patient and enduring," remarked one of the company.

"Patient as a Christian—enduring as a martyr," was answered. "Poor man! He was worthy of a better fate. He ought to have succeeded, for he deserved success."

"Did he not succeed?" questioned the one who had spoken of his patience and endurance.

"No, sir. He died poor, as I have just said. Nothing that he put his hand to ever succeeded. A strange fatality seemed to attend every enterprise."

"I was with him in his last moments," said the other, "and I thought he died rich."

"No. He has left nothing behind," was replied. "The heirs will have no concern as to the administration of his estate."

"He left a good name," said one, "and that is something."

"And a legacy of noble deeds that were done in the name of humanity," remarked another.

"And precious examples," said a third.

"Lessons of patience in suffering; of hope in adversity; of heavenly confidence, when no sunbeams fell upon his bewildering path," was the testimony of another.

"And high truths, manly courage, heroic fortitude."

"Then he died rich!" was the emphatic declaration. "Richer than the millionaire who went to his long home on the same day, a miserable pauper in all but gold. A sad funeral, did you say? No, my friend, it was, rather, a triumphal procession! Not the burial of a human clod, but the ceremonials attendant on the translation of an angel. Did not succeed! Why, his whole life was a series of successes. In every conflict he came off the victor, and now the victor's crown is on his brow. Any grasping, soulless, selfish man, with a moderate share of brains, may gather in money, and learn the art of keeping it; but not one in a hundred can bravely conquer in the battle of life as Edmonson has conquered, and step forth from the ranks of men, a Christian hero. No, no; he did not die poor, but rich—rich in neighborly love, and rich in celestial affections. And his heirs have an interest in the adminisiration of his estate. A large property has been left, and let them see to it that they do not lose precious things through false estimates and ignorant depreciations."

"You have a new way of estimating the wealth of a man," said the one who had first expressed sympathy for the deceased.

"Is it not the right way?" was answered. "There are higher things to gain in this world, than wealth that perishes. Riches of priceless value ever reward the true merchant, who trades for wisdom, buying it with the silver of truth and the gold of love. He dies rich who can take his treasure with him to the new land where he is to abide forever, and he who has to leave all behind on which he has placed affection, dies poor indeed. Our friend Edmonson died richer than a Girard or an Astor; his monument is built of good deeds and noble examples. It will abide forever."

XIII.

CURSED WITH BLESSINGS.

"Cursed with blessings." I closed the page, and leaned back in reflection.

"Here is another paradox," said I. "Cursed with blessings! It is simply a contradiction in terms. What does the writer mean?"

I turned to the page again, and read on. "There is such a thing as being cursed with blessings, so that the earthly good a man seeks, shall become the greatest evil that can be visited upon him."

Some gleams of light passed into my mind. Thought and memory went to work; and soon around the proposition gathered a host of illustrating incidents. I remembered the case of a man who, in early and middle life, always, in family prayer, brought in the petition—"Increase our basket and store." And the worldly good things he so much desired, came; came in rich abundance.

He added house to house, until his rents flowed back upon him, a princely income. But, his selfish heart made all his earthly blessings a curse. Like the miser, his life was in his possessions; and when anything threatened these, trouble of spirit arose. The dread of loss by fire, haunted him like a murderer's conscience. He insured; but felt only half protected by insurance, for there were dishonest companies, flaws in contracts, quibbles in the law. He had suffered one loss in this way. It was not serious, but enough to break his faith in Insurance as a reliable protection against fire. And so, every stroke of the alarm bell, by night or by day, gave a shock to his nerves, and sent a pang of fear to his heart. Sweet, refreshing sleep, became a stranger to his pillow. The ghost of apprehension was forever by his side, a fearful vision.

Then came a morbid dread of poverty; and, after a time, his day-dreams and fitful night-visions began to be of pauperism and the almshouse. At sixty he was insane, from this cause, and died, in the hallucination of abject want, leaving a hundred thousand dollars of property, which passed to heirs, who made the blessing a curse also, as he had done, but in another way. In five years from his death, his two sons realized their father's fears, and now fill paupers' graves.

"Cursed with blessings! Even so!" I said, as memory closed the page on which this history was recorded. "Like the manna which the children of Israel gathered in the wilderness, life's blessings must be used to-day—if hoarded selfishly, they will not keep."

Another illustration memory gave. I knew a man who set his heart upon wealth, as a means of comfort in old age. "I am willing to work now," he used to say, "while I am young and vigorous; though business is distasteful to me. I love ease and freedom, and for the sake of gaining them, I toil on in early manhood."

And while he toiled on he was comparatively happy. I can remember him as one of the most cheerful men in my circle of acquaintance. But competence rewarded his labor ere yet his sun of life had swept beyond the zenith, and his "basket and store" were full. His toil crowned him with blessings. And so he retired from the busy world to enjoy these good things which had come to him in return for useful industry. Alas for my friend! He had no taste for books, no love of art, no fondness for country life, or pleasant gardening. His mind had been educated only in one direction. He was a man of business, and that alone. And so, he had nothing to do but to sit down and enjoy himself. How impossible that was, he discovered in less than a month. During the first and second seasons he tried Cape May, Saratoga, Newport, and a trip down the Lakes and the St. Lawrence. But he did not really enjoy himself. How could he? There is no enjoyment for a man living without a purpose. Mere killing time is only a slow, soul-killing operation, and is always accompanied by pain.

Ten years ago it was when my friend retired from business, to enjoy his fortune. His cup of blessing was full, and he has been holding it to his lips ever since, trying to find sweetness in the draught; but, judging from the expression of his face, the tone of his voice, and the character of his remarks, I think the wine in his cup must be dashed with unusual bitterness. His blessing has become a curse.

Another received a moderate fortune from a distant relative. He happened to be heir-at-law, and the relative dying without a will, he came most unexpectedly into possession of about thirty-five thousand dollars in cash. He was a clerk, with a salary of one thousand dollars a year, living frugally with his wife and two children in a small, rented house. Few men enjoyed life with a keener zest than this young man. But the fortune proved his ruin. The clerkship was at once given up for a business venture; the hired house for a handsome purchased dwelling; omnibus rides for drives in an elegant carriage; social tea companies for elegant parties. His course was brilliant but brief. The blessing was made a curse. Soured, dissatisfied, maddened by a sudden fall from the height up to which he had soared, away down into the valley of abject poverty, he lost self-respect and self-control. Drink made the ruin complete. His pale widow sits toiling now, early and late, striving to keep the wolf of hunger from her door.

Shall we go on, varying these illustrations of the text? They may be taken from every condition in life, and from all of its wide relations. There is not a reader who cannot supply his quota, and set them even in stronger light than we have done. And there is not a reader who may not, with the writer, find in his own past history almost unnumbered instances, in which he has turned his good things into evil; his blessing into cursing. We all do it, when we let affection rest in mere natural and sensual things, instead of making these things ministers of the soul's higher life. Worldly possessions are blessings, if acquired as a means to useful ends; but they curse us, when we make them our chiefest good.

XIV.

HE THAT OVERCOMETH.

"You will be at the meeting to-night," said a clergyman to an influential member of his society, speaking in an affirmative voice.

"No," was the decisive answer; "I shall remain at home."

"Why so, Mr. Percival?" asked the clergyman, manifesting surprise.

"It is better for me to stay away."

"I don't understand you."

"I am too excitable. The way in which some of our members speak and act in these church meetings chafes and annoys me to such a degree that I lose temper, and say things that do harm rather than good; so I have concluded to stay at home, and let matters take their course."

"Is that right, brother Percival?" The minister looked at his parishioner with a sober countenance.

"It is best," was answered.

"Best for what?"

"Best for my peace of mind, at least."

"Even though disorderly measures are carried in your absence, and the church sustains an injury in consequence?"

"I am not so sure that such will be the case," Mr. Percival answered.

"There is an important measure to be sustained or abandoned this evening."

"I know."

"You are in the affirmative?"

"I am."

"And you consider this measure of vital importance to the church?"

"I do."

"And yet deliberately propose an abandonment of your post of duty?"

"I am not fit to take the post of duty. My temper is too excitable."

The minister gazed for some moments into the face of Mr. Percival, and then said—

"I was reading to-day in the book of Revelations, and noted a certain passage as involving a most important doctrine. It was this: 'To him that *overcometh* will I give to eat of the tree of life.' I read on, and soon the same doctrine was repeated, but with a new assurance—'He that *overcometh* shall not be hurt of the second death.' Still I read, and again the doctrine was announced, in the words, 'He that *overcometh*, the same shall be clothed in white raiment; and I will not blot out his name out of the book of life.' Now, what is it that we are to overcome in order that we may 'eat of the tree of life,' and 'not be hurt of the second death.' Think, my dear brother, and answer this question in your own heart."

"We must overcome evil," replied Mr. Percival, after a pause. His voice was rather sober.

"This impulsive temper of which you complain," said the minister, "is certainly an evil, if it hinders your usefulness to such a degree as to keep you away from duty."

Mr. Percival bent his head, while a shade of concern passed over his features.

"Is not the way plain before you, my brother?" The promise of life eternal is to him that *overcometh*. You must overcome if you would not be hurt of the second death."

"Is it not far better," said Mr. Percival, "knowing this weakness of nature, to keep myself free from temptation."

"Will that be a conquest of evil?" The cowardly soldier might offer the same reason for not venturing into battle, lest he disgrace himself, and injure his country, by running away. No, no; this will not do. You must conquer the foes of heaven upon the battle-field of your own heart. You must *overcome*."

Mr. Percival bent his head again, and did not answer.

"Go to this meeting to-night," said the clergyman, after a brief silence. "Go to do your duty; and in the divine strength, that will surely be given to you, if you strive for victory over your easily-besetting sin, will you conquer and stand up a man. Go. A good cause has need of your best efforts."

"I thank you for this wise counsel," replied Mr. Percival. "I see that you are right. I must not let this sin, that doth so easily beset me, hold me back, a coward, from my place, when God calls me to stand up for the right. I must overcome, and, God helping me, I will."

"Now you are in the right spirit," said the minister, encouragingly. "Hold fast to this good purpose, and go in this state of heavenly trust. You will return from the meeting to-night a stronger and a happier man."

Under this view of the case, Mr. Percival could not absent himself from the church-meeting. But he went with a guard set over his feelings, and a bridle on his tongue. There was one member who always led an opposition, no matter what the subject under consideration. It was only necessary to make a move towards doing something, to insure objection; and as he was a cool talker, and had a great deal of self-possession, he generally managed to carry a party with him. Towards this individual, whose name was Larned, Mr. Percival did not entertain very kind feelings; and whenever he opposed him, it was with excitement of manner, and, too often, with intemperance of speech. Thus he lost influence in his opposition; and always came away from such meetings deeply mortified at his want of self-control.

The business of the evening had progressed almost to a conclusion, without a remark from Mr. Percival, who sat a little apart from the rest, so quiet and absorbed that few thought him at all interested in the subject under discussion. Mr.

Larned, as usual, was in the opposition, and his cool, specious way of talking had gained over to his side quite a large number of the superficial minds in the assembly, and there was danger of defeat to a cause, the advocates of which had only the best interests of religion in view. The minister and others glanced towards Mr. Percival; but he neither moved nor looked up. At last, the vote was about being taken. Then, and not till then, did the excitable member, who saw the whole subject in the clearest light, venture to take the floor. He did so with a prayer on his lips—a prayer for aid in his struggle for self-control. His voice trembled a little as he began, and those who knew him well expected soon the old vehemence, and intemperance of manner. But a new spirit was at work in the heart of Mr. Percival, which soon showed itself in even tones, and a deliberate enunciation. He took up the subject under consideration, and presented it in so many new lights, that numbers who had regarded it as of minor importance, now saw it as a measure which it was clearly their duty to support. He finished, without a single unkind word, sharp invective, or angry denunciation.

It was the usual course of things for Mr. Larned

to reply to Mr. Percival's hot speech, in his cool, semi-sarcastic way, and neutralize, with a large number, all that was really valuable in what he had said. The contrast between his manner and that of Mr. Percival, no one saw more plainly than did Mr. Percival himself; who also perceived, but when too late, that he owed defeat to his own quick, blinding temper.

Now, however, Mr. Larned, on rising to answer the forcibly stated argument of Mr. Percival, found himself without power. There had been no intemperate warmth; no blundering confusion of ideas; but a calm, rational directness of speech, that carried conviction to almost every mind—not excepting that of the always opposing member. When the question was taken, the measure passed by an almost unanimous vote.

"The first fruits, my brother," said the minister, as he walked away from the meeting with Mr. Percival. "And if they be of such goodly size and quality, in the beginning, what may we not expect from the full grown tree. You have done nobly—nobly. 'He that is slow to anger is better than the mighty; and he that ruleth his spirit, than he that taketh a city.'"

"It was a hard struggle," answered Mr. Percival,

more in humility than exultation. "A very hard struggle. I so dreaded, knowing my infirmity, to take the floor, that nothing but an overpowering sense of duty could have driven me to my feet. I saw the whole subject in clear light, and all the arguments in its favor were on my tongue's end. But I feared the blinding influence of a hasty temper. Thank Heaven! I was able to overcome in the struggle."

"And so accomplished a double good," said the minister. "Good for yourself, and good for a cause that needed your advocacy. And now, my brother," added the minister, "let the valuable lesson this night received, go with you through life. Never shrink from duty because of fear lest you are not equal to the struggle against natural evil, which may be required. The Christian must overcome natural evil. Must put down the strong man of sin. Must succeed in every struggle with wrong. We must be conquerors here, if we would receive the victor's crown hereafter.. *He that overcometh shall not be hurt of the second death.*"

XV.

THE TRIALS OF A DAY.

BABY had not slept well; and the mother, robbed during the night of her refreshing slumber, awoke later than usual in the morning. Her first sensations were of lassitude and exhaustion—her first consciousness, that of being behind time for the day. She started up as soon as she was fairly awake, with a hurried feeling, and commenced dressing herself in haste; but scarcely had she left her bed before the baby missed her, and commenced crying to be taken up. Her husband, Mr. Samuel Jenkins, who liked to indulge in a quiet morning nap, was disturbed by this untimely and, to his ears, very discordant, music, and spoke out rather sharply to the baby, which frightened her, and set her to crying with increased violence.

"Why don't you take her up, Jane?" growled the half-asleep and half-awake husband.

"I will when I'm dressed," replied Mrs. Jenkins with manifest irritation.

"Then dress in double quick time. This din is horrible!" said Mr. Jenkins, who was a rough sort of a man, though well meaning in a general way.

Poor Mrs. Jenkins was not helped by this in the smallest degree. Her hands shook, and her knees trembled, as she hurried on her garments, and drew them together. Baby's screams increased in power up to the moment the last pin was inserted, and did not cease until lifted from the bed and held tightly against her mother's bosom. The pale face, that bent itself down until it touched the face of the little one, was now wet with tears. The mother felt weak and discouraged.

Mrs. Jenkins had recently become a church member, and was trying to regulate her life by the pure precepts of religion. Her husband, on the other hand, cared for little beyond his business; and sought for the accomplishments of nothing besides the merest natural ends. The boundaries of this world limited his hopes and aspirations. In the main, he was a kind husband, and, in the estimation of his neighbors, "a good sort of a man, but wide awake to his own interests." Mr. Jenkins had not yet learned to think out of himself, as it were, nor to calculate with accuracy the effect of his words and conduct upon others. The consequence was, that he was all the time doing or saying something that hurt or shadowed the feelings of his wife, who was sensitive. In his rough speech and imperative demand about the baby, Mr. Jenkins did not feel half the ill nature that to his wife was expressed in his voice and manner, and was wholly unconscious of the jar and pain they occasioned.

As Mrs. Jenkins sat with her tearful face pressed down upon the face of her now quiet baby, she endeavored to lift her heart upwards in a prayer for strength to endure patiently the trials of her life; but, even while the petition quivered on her lips, a call from waking children in the next room drew back her thoughts, and gave another jar to her feelings; for the call was made in fretful voices, accompanied by the too-well known signs of contention. The sudden start she gave sent a pain through her head.

"Oh, dear!" sighed the mother, "my strength is not equal to my burdens. If I felt well and strong, it would be different; but, in my weak state, how can I keep up?—How can I do my duty?"

"Mother!" called the loud, angry voice of a little girl, "make Anna give me my stocking!"

"I hav'n't got her stocking!" retorted Anna, in even a louder and more ear-shocking voice.

"You have, I say! Now give it to me this minute!"

"It is not yours! I won't!"

"Mother!"

"Good gracious, Jane!" exclaimed Mr. Jenkins, starting up in bed, "why don't you stop that quarrelling? It's dreadful!"

Mrs. Jenkins did not reply to her husband, although a cutting retort came to her lips, but went immediately into the next room to restore harmony, if possible. She found her two little girls struggling together for the possession of a stocking that each claimed. To punish them both on the spot, was the first impulse of her mind; and she had even raised her hand, in sudden anger, to strike, when better counsels prevailed.

"I must control myself, as a Christian woman," she said, "or I cannot control them."

And so she held back resolutely her excited feelings, and merely uttered, with forced calmness, yet in grave rebuke, the names of her children. The two little girls were passive instantly. There was something in the tone and look of their mother which they felt no inclination to oppose. It went past their external strife of feeling, and calmed the inner turbulence at once.

"Now, let me see the stocking." She spoke in a low, but serious voice.

Anna placed the stocking in her mother's hand. Mrs. Jenkins looked at it for a moment, and then held it close to the eyes of the little girl.

"Whose stocking is that, Anna?" she asked steadily.

"Mary's," answered the child, crimsoning, and hanging down her head.

"You said just now it was yours."

"I thought it was."

"I think I heard you call Mary a bad name. Was that right?"

"No, ma'am," answered the child, subdued by the calmness of her mother's exterior.

"Why did you call her that name?"

"I was angry," said Anna.

"And hardly knew what you were saying or doing?"

"I don't think I did, mother. But I'm sorry;

and if you'll forgive me, I'll ask Mary's pardon, for I was most to blame."

Now Mrs. Jenkins was really taken by surprise at this confession and repentance on the part of the passionate, self-willed child, whose passion and self-will she had so often tried in vain to subdue and control; but never with so strong a hand upon her own feelings as now. Her voice trembled a little as she answered—

"Mary is not altogether blameless. She permitted angry feelings to disturb her heart, and harsh words to fall from her tongue. I do not, therefore, think that she will permit you to ask her pardon; for she has sinned also—sinned against that good God, whose loving angels have been round your pillows all the night, protecting you from evil. How much better would it have been, my children, if your voices had been lifted in a hymn of thanksgiving. You have made me feel sad—very sad."

By this time all resentment had died out of the children's hearts, and the almost mournful voice of their mother filled them with sorrow and regret.

"Love each other as God has loved you," said Mrs. Jenkins, kissing her little girls. Tears fell over her cheeks, for her feelings were touched and softened.

"Don't cry, mother! don't cry!" urged Anna and Mary, throwing their small white arms around her neck. "We'll be good! We won't quarrel any more. Don't cry!"

Again the mother kissed her children, saying—

"If you will love each other, I shall be happy."

"Oh, we will, mother! we will!" exclaimed Anna; "and we'll help you so much. I'll dress myself as quickly as I can, and hold dear little Eddy for you."

"Thank you, dear! That will be so nice!" answered the mother.

"And I'll go down and help about setting the table," said Mary. "I can put on the plates and the napkins, and the knives and forks."

"What smart little girls I have!" was the mother's encouraging answer. "You shall do all that, Mary. So make haste and get on your clothes. But, remember, the hair must be nicely brushed, and everything about you as neat as a new pin. My dining-room girl must be the pink of tidiness."

Singularly enough, when Mrs. Jenkins thought about her head-ache, it was gone; and so was the extreme lassitude from which she had suffered on rising. A new life seemed coursing through her veins; and she was half in wonder at the change.

"Set baby on the bed, mother," said Anna. "I can play with him and dress too."

"I'm afraid he will cry, and disturb your father."

"No, he won't. Set him down. I'll keep him laughing, instead of crying; see if I don't."

The baby felt, also, the new sphere that was pervading the room. He did not resist when his mother attempted to place him on the bed, and made no objection to being left alone with Anna.

So that first trial of the day was passed through, and Mrs. Jenkins, in endeavoring to meet it in a better spirit than usual, had risen above the darkness, the irritation, and oppressive weakness that seemed as if they would bear her down to the very earth. Even physical pain and exhaustion had disappeared under the influence of a new condition of mind. Mary soon followed her mother down stairs, and aided, with cheerfulness and alacrity, in setting the breakfast table, and putting things in order. She was a bright little girl, and only needed a calmly controlling will, and a wisely directing hand, to make her orderly and useful. It was the same with Anna, who, though quick-tempered, had good impulses.

Mr. Jenkins, who had been wakened by the baby's loud crying, and a second time roused from pleasant morning slumbers, by the angry strife of Anna and Mary, heard, half in wonder, the calm words which his wife had addressed to the children, who, in his regard, deserved summary punishment, to begin with, and talking to afterwards. He knew that his wife's mind was interested on the subject of religion, and that she had become a church member; but the change in her manner, since attaching herself to the church, had not been altogether agreeable to him. Her old lightness of spirit had departed, and her feelings seemed all the while shadowed. If he spoke to her a little roughly, as he had been in the habit of doing, tears would come into her eyes.

"If this religion," said he, "is going to fill my house with gloom, if sadness is to sit forever on the face of my wife, I shall do my best to banish it from our dwelling."

But this little evidence of the better spirit that was at work in the heart of his wife, changed materially the aspect of the case. Before, she had repressed, with a strong hand, all strife between her children; subduing the external manifestation of anger, but not changing the evil condition of mind. The storm of *her* passion only obliterated the external signs of *theirs*. The ill nature, the unkindness, the hate, were all alive, and ever gaining strength under the unwise repression. Now, what a change a few calm sentences had produced!

When Mr. Jenkins came down at breakfast-time, and looked across the table at his wife, he saw that her face was paler than usual.

"Are you not well, Anna?" he inquired, in a tone of unusual interest.

She smiled back upon him a sudden smile that made her face look beautiful, as of old, in his eyes.

"Eddy was wakeful, and I slept but poorly last night," she answered. "But I feel as well as usual, and better than when I got up this morning."

"How nicely the table looks," said Mr. Jenkins, glancing around, with a pleased manner. "Have you got a new girl?"

"I'm the new girl," spoke out Mary, too much gratified by this commendation to keep silent.

"You? Why bless my heart! Is that so?" answered the father, affecting an air of surprise.

"Yes; Mary is the new girl; and you don't know how handy she is—"

"And you've got a new nurse too, if I'm not mistaken." Mr. Jenkins glanced at Anna. "Now, that's something like, my little dears," he added; "and I'm more pleased to think you've been helping your mother this morning, than if I'd found a purse of gold."

What a glow of pleasure warmed every breast! What happy smiles sat on every countenance.

"But, come Jane," added Mr. Jenkins, "pour out my coffee, and let me get through with breakfast. You're late this morning, by nearly half an hour. I felt strongly tempted to get impatient and scold; but you were all doing your best, and so cheerfully, too, that I hadn't the heart to be ill-natured. I won't promise for to-morrow morning, however."

"You mustn't be too hard on me, dear," Mrs. Jenkins answered, with a faint smile, and a voice, whose pleading softness went right to her husband's heart. "Eddy don't sleep very well, you know, and I'm broken of a good many hours' rest every night. So, if I get sound asleep towards morning, and lie a little too late, I ought to be forgiven. The spirit is willing, but the flesh is weak."

Mr. Jenkins couldn't just stand that. It kind of choked him.

"I won't scold again, if you lie until dinner time!" He answered, with sudden feeling. "I'll get up myself, and with Mary's help, cook the breakfast if needed. How thoughtless we strong, hearty men are, sometimes," he added. "We don't consider as we should, the broken rest, and shattered nerves of our wives. And, now that I think of it," he went on—"it does seem to me, that scolding and ill-nature are rather out of place in our home. There is a better way for us to get along, I am sure. You taught me that, Jane, this morning; and the lesson, I think will abide."

"Me? How? Where?" Mrs. Jenkins looked across the table half in wonder

"I will tell you another time," he replied, as his eyes wandered from the face of his wife to Anna and Mary. She understood him then; and a new hope sprung up in her heart, and a new strength pervaded her spirit.

"If a single effort at self-control has worked such great results as these," said Mrs. Jenkins to herself, "what may I not hope to accomplish in time? God help me to overcome the selfish inclinings of my heart!"

Mr. Jenkins left his home on that morning, with a new set of thoughts active in his mind; and a new impression of his wife's character.

"If religion have done that," he said, speaking to himself, "then it is worth something. I've never had much faith in this singing and praying; and never fancied these solemn faces. What I want to see are reformed men and women. Religion isn't worth a copper if it doesn't change the life as well as the heart."

All very well for Mr. Jenkins. He belonged to a class.

The next trial of the day for Mrs. Jenkins approached. The getting of Anna and Mary off to school had been always attended with trouble. Neither of them liked school very well; and both were in the habit of conjuring up every difficulty in their power, and worrying their mother until her stock of patience was exhausted. The scene not unfrequently closed with a passionate outbreak on the mother's part, accompanied by blows, when the children were driven forth in tears.

Mrs. Jenkins, now that this trial was near, began to experience a pressure on her feelings. Her little girls had behaved very well, so far, and been a great help to her; and, in consideration of this and as a reward, she thought for a moment, of letting them stay at home on that day. But, she saw at once, the error and weakness of this. It was merely getting around, or evading a duty, not meeting it in the true spirit. So, she schooled her own heart to calmness, and when the time came for Anna and Mary to get ready, she said, in a quiet, firm way, yet smiling as she spoke:

"What next? Time is passing?"

Anna and Mary looked at their mother. They understood her; and she saw in their manner, that the thought of school was an unpleasant one.

"I haven't seen my little girls as happy as they have been this morning for a long time," she said, holding their eyes in her own steady gaze. "But the reason is plain. The proverb says: 'To be good is to be happy.' You have been good—that is, useful to your mother and kind to one another; and so happiness has flowed into your hearts from your Father in heaven, who is the source of all true happiness. Continue to be good —that is to do right, and the Lord, who loves you, will fill your hearts with pleasure. Now, what is your next right action?"

"To go to school," replied Anna with promptness.

"Come!" said Mary, catching hold of her sister's hand, "let us get ready in a minute, and not give mother a bit of trouble. I know where all my things are."

And the two children tripped away as lightly as if they were about making ready for a pleasure party instead of school. In a few minutes, they came down, playful as kittens, and after kissing their mother and the baby, went laughing, instead crying, off to school.

"Isn't this wonderful!" said Mrs. Jenkins, as the door closed on the children. "Oh, the power of true thoughts and right purposes! I am in amazement at these large results from such small efforts. It was not so very hard to control myself; not so very hard to speak calmly, and firmly, and with love, instead of anger, in my tones. Dear children! Has not your mother been most to blame for your ill-tempers, and selfish activities? O Lord"—and heart and voice went upwards,—"help me to conquer myself—to do right and to be right. Oh. be strength in my weakness. Give me patience, long suffering, and unselfish love!"

With what a new spirit, with what an elevation of feeling, with what cheerful hope, did Mrs. Jenkins move through her household duties during the morning of that day! No pain nor weakness depressed her body, and no despondency her mind; though her trials were far greater than usual, arising from the fact that she had no domestic in the family, she was able to meet and overcome the many difficulties of her position with an ease that astonished herself.

Dinner time brought home her hungry little girls and their father. They came in together; Mary crying out as she entered the door—

"Oh, dear mother, I'm 'most starved! Isn't dinner ready? No! I declare!" Her eyes had reached forward into the little dining-room, and discovered that the table was not even set. "It's too bad! And I'm so hungry! Can't I have some bread and butter?"

"Why, Jane!" said Mr. Jenkins, a frown darkening his face. "How could you neglect things so? If you can't have meals ready in time, there is no use in coming home to them. My business won't wait."

Now this was breaking in upon Mrs. Jenkins rather roughly, and the sudden jar came near throwing her spirit from its even balance. But, from a quick sense of fear, she rallied herself, and, with a smile on her lips, said to her husband, in an even, penetrating voice—

"Don't be too hard on me, dear. Remember, I have no girl. Be a little patient, and I'll promise to have a good dinner on the table in ten minutes by the watch. I've been doing my best."

"Not a word more, Jane," answered Mr. Jenkins. "I stand rebuked. Ten minutes won't signify, here nor there. I know you've done your best, as you always do."

"Can't I have some bread and butter?" Mary jerked at her mother's dress, and cried out in a very cross way.

"I'll tell you what you can have, my child," said Mrs. Jenkins, in a pleasant tone of voice.

"What, mother?" Anna's face brightened little.

"The pleasure of helping me as you did this morning. You know you are my little waiting-maid. It is late, and father is in a hurry for his dinner. Move around quickly, and get the table set, while I see to dishing up the meat and vegetables."

Mary sprang away to the dining-room, and soon the air was musical with the rattle of plates, and the jingle of knives, forks, and spoons; while Mrs. Jenkins, with lightened feelings, went into the kitchen to take up the dinner. In less than ten minutes the dinner-bell rung.

"Well, that is quick work!" said Mr. Jenkins, as he sat down to the table. "There must have been some magic in the case."

He looked particularly well pleased.

"I'll try to be up to the minute to-morrow," answered Mrs. Jenkins. "But if I fail a little, you must all help me by your patience. It does me a world of good. It is not from willful neglect that I am behindhand in anything."

Mrs. Jenkins did not mean to rebuke her husband; but, what she then said, he felt as a reproof. His eyes were opened to a juster estimate of his wife, to a higher appreciation of her character, and to his own spirit of selfish exaction. How different all would have been if, instead of exercising Christian patience, Mrs. Jenkins had permitted, as she had often done before, wounded feelings to blind, and passion to destroy, her self-control. And she had her reward in a tranquil spirit, and in a humble self-approval.

The evening of that day, which opened with such evil promise, closed peacefully for the household of Mr. Jenkins.

"How did you manage to work such a wonderful transformation in yourself, in the children, and even in your husband," said Mr. Jenkins, as he leaned towards his wife across the little sewing-table. The children were all in bed and asleep, and they sat alone, talking of the day's incidents, trials, and conquests. "It seems to me almost like a dream."

"Not in my own strength, dear husband" replied Mrs. Jenkins, her voice trembling, and her eyes glistening with tears. "I never felt weaker, or more unfitted for the day's trials, than I did this morning. I had lost sleep with Eddy, and when I awoke, I felt so weak and nervous that I could scarcely rise. Before I had dressed myself, a headache set in. Baby screamed; husband scolded; Anna and Mary quarrelled. I felt that the trial was beyond my strength—and so it was. In my weakness and despair, I looked up and prayed for patience, wisdom, and endurance; and God helped me in my extremity. He gave me patience, self-control, and wisdom, for right action. Of myself, I had no power for good; in Him, I have overcome the enemies that sought to destroy my peace."

Mr. Jenkins let his eyes fall from the earnest face of his wife, and for some moments looked down upon the floor.

"If that is what you call religion, Jane," he said, looking up, "I think the more the world has of it the better. It does not contain a single element of sadness; but, on the contrary, banishes gloom, and scatters good deeds and sunshine all around. If it has carried you, cheerfully, through a day commenced in such dark promise, what a blessed life-companion it must be! I understand now what religion really is; what trust in the Lord is; what prayer for divine strength means."

"May he give you that strength, my husband," said Mrs. Jenkins, fervently. "Oh, look up to Him, and he will aid you in trial, and in temptation, as he has aided me. Let us walk together in this new way. Let us help one another."

Mr. Jenkins gave his hand to his wife, and, as he felt its eager clasp, he answered—

"Teach and lead me by your sweet example, Jane, as you have taught me to-day. I may not be a very rapid scholar, but I will be learning something all the while, if you will but look past my roughness and hardness, which is more on the surface than in the heart, and still keep repeating your lessons, though the scholar be dull, and, at times, rebellious. You shall have your reward in the end."

And Mr. Jenkins was right. She *had* her reward. Years afterwards she would look back and bless the trials of that first day of truly Christian warfare. Her conquests then were only the beginning of a series of conquests over the evils of her nature. Daily, as she entered into her duties, and performed them from a principle of religion, did she gain new power, and rise into higher states of enjoyment. The circle of her life seemed ever sweeping in ascending spirals. How beautifully and effectively, did the Christian wife and mother illustrate the doctrine she professed, by an untiring devotion of herself to the good of her husband and children! From them she had honor and love. Best of all, in her eyes, was their daily growth into the likeness and image of God, through self-denials, patience, repression of evil, and good deeds done in the name of charity. Yes, she had her reward, and it was given in rich abundance.

XVI.

ANGEL VISITS.

They do not always visit us in beautiful garments,making the air golden with their sunny smiles. Oftener, they come in sober-hued vestments, with lips grief-curved, and eyes heavy, as from weeping. But, come to us when and how they will, it is ever in love. Daily they are about our paths, though we perceive them not with our dull bodily senses; nor even recognize their presence by the spirit's finer instincts—for, "of the earth earthy," as we are, and with affections clinging to the earth, we have neither eyes nor ears for the inner sights and inner voices which are for the pure in heart. Yes, they are about our daily paths, smoothing and making them flowery when they may; but oftener piling up obstructions and making them rough and thorny.

"Rough and thorny! Piling up obstructions!"

we hear from the lips of some life-weary sufferer. "Is this a work for angels?"

Beautiful seemed the way before you, in the bright morning of early womanhood, heart-sick and life-weary one! And as your eyes went far onward, how many lovely vistas opened, showing blessed Arcadias in the smiling distance! To gain them was, you felt, to gain heaven; and onward you pressed with eager footsteps. You did not gain them! For a while, the path was even, and the fragrance of a hundred blossoms delighted your senses. But all at once your feet were wounded—there were sharp obstructions in the way; then thick clouds and darkness were before you, hiding the lovely Eden. Still, you pressed onward, though the way was rough, and the sunny vistas opening to the land of promise, were hidden from your straining vision. Then a mountain arose suddenly, whose rocky steeps you could not climb. Despair was in your heart; and in the bitterness of your disappointment you called yourself one mocked of God.

It was not so, precious immortal! Not so, pilgrim to a better land than the Arcadia of your maiden dreams! At the very foot of that inaccessible mountain, a narrow path became visible; and though it looked rough and had no green margin, beautiful with flowers, there was an emotion of thankfulness in your heart for even this way of escape: for, already a mortal dread had seized upon your spirit. With hurrying footsteps you entered this new way, and the hope that it would quickly lead around the mountain, and bring the sunny land again in view, repressed the fear that else had been paralyzing.

It was the hand of an angel which led you into that new way, and kept your heart from fainting. Narrow, rough and flowerless though it proved, it was a better way than that along which you were passing with such buoyant steps—for it bent heavenward. And think, life-weary one!—do you not feel that you are nearer heaven now than when the sun of this world shone from an unclouded sky above the path of pleasure and prosperity? Think, and answer to yourself the question.

A heart-stricken mother sat grieving for the loss of her youngest-born, the sweetest and loveliest of her precious flock—grieving and refusing to be comforted. There had been loving sympathy, gentle remonstrance, and pious teaching from the lips of the minister who had a year before touched the forehead of her babe with the waters of baptism; but all availed not—the fountain of tears stayed not its waters, nor was the murmuring voice hushed in her rebellious spirit. At length, one came to her who had known a like sorrow, and whose heart had, even like hers, been bowed into the very dust. She took into her own soft hand the passive hand of the mourner, which gave not back a sign. A little while she held it, clasping her fingers in a gentle pressure; then in a voice whose tender modulations went vibrating to the inmost of her spirit, she said:

"You had an angel visit last night."

An angel visit! What did the words signify?

"Only a year has passed since I had a like visit," continued the friend. "I did not recognize the heavenly messenger when she came, for my eyes were too full of tears to see her radiant form. She came and went, bearing on her bosom as she passed upward to the regions of eternal sunshine, the spirit of my lovely boy!"

The hand of the mourner answered to the light pressure of that in which it lay. That night, went on the comforter, "I saw in a dream—I call it a dream, but regard it as a revelation—my translated one among the blessed in the upper kingdom of our Father. He was in the arms of the angel-mother, whose love for him it was plain to see was wise and tender, surpassing all my own deep affection, as far as the unselfish love of an angel surpasses the love of a weak and erring creature of earth.

"'Grieve no more!' said the heavenly being, as she came to me. 'I have not taken this innocent one from you in anger or cruelty, but in love—love for both the mother and child. As for him, he is safe in his celestial home for ever, and is and will be blessed far above anything you could ask—for it hath not entered into the heart of even a mother to conceive what transcendent delights are in store for those who are born into heaven. Is it not, therefore, better for your child? Were I to say, take him again into the cold, dark world of sorrow, sin and suffering, would you bear him back? No, grieving mother, no! You love this precious one too well. But, how is it better for you to lose the child in whom your heart was so bound up? I see the question on your lips, and answer,—That is always best which lifts the spirit nearest to God. Is it not so? Think! Not with a heavenly, but with an earthly and selfish affection, did you love your child, and such an affection can not truly bless either you or your babe. It is now in heaven, and as your heart follows it there, it will come into heavenly associations, and thus be filled with aspirations for that higher life which descends from and bears back its recipient into heaven. Grieving one! I came to you in mercy; and though tears have followed my visit, they are falling on good seeds planted in your heart.'

"Thus spoke to me that angel-mother of my child, and ever since, her words have been my stay and comfort. Such an angel came to you last night, grieving friend. The visit was in love, not in anger. Then lift your eyes upward, and no longer permit them to rest on the gloomy grave. The spirit of your child has already arisen, more beautiful in form, and is now with the angels appointed for its guardianship. The wiser love of our good Father hath transplanted a flower of earth to blossom in the warmer atmosphere of heaven. Be thankful, then, dear friend. Oh, be thanful!—but weep not!"

And the heart, which no words of consolation had been able to reach, felt itself swelling with a deep emotion, and lifting itself upwards towards the All-merciful.

"I will believe that it was an angel who came here last night and bore away my child," she whispered, as with shut eyes, fringed by tear-gemmed lashes, she bowed her head upon the bosom of her consoler. "Oh, if anything can soothe the anguish of this bereavement, it is to know that my precious babe, for whom I have cared so tenderly, passed from my arms to those of an angel; and that he was thus borne safely across the dark valley into which I looked down with such a heart-shudder. I bless you for speaking such words of consolation!"

Not alone in misfortune or bereavement do angels visit us. They do not always make the way rough, nor always darken the fires around which we gather. Daily they come to us; hourly they seek to draw nearer, and quicken our better impulses. A thousand evils—soul-destroying evils—are warded off by them, even though we are unconscious of their presence, and, it may be, resist the very influences by which such priceless benefits are conferred.

"Ah!" we hear it said, "if we could but open

our eyes and see; if the scales that obstruct our inner vision could be removed; if we could know our celestial visitors when they come!"

We may know them, and we may perceive their presence. Whether we are in prosperity or in adversity, in joy or in sorrow, angel visitors are with us whenever the thought goes upward, and the heart yearns for a better life. Their mission to the sons of men is to draw them heavenward; and if sorrow, affliction, or adversity is needed for the accomplishment of this great end, they are made subservient in the good work. But when, in their high mission, they bow a thirsty soul to the bitter waters of Marah, their hands hold not back the healing branch; and a song of rejoicing is soon heard instead of lamentation. Elim, with its twelve wells of water and seventy palm-trees, is just beyond.

Happy is that spirit to which the angels come not on their errands of mercy in vain!

XVII.

ALGERNON, THE MERCHANT.

The day closed, and Algernon, the merchant, turned thoughtfully from his counting-room, and took his way homeward. Almost without intermission, since morning, had he been absorbed in his money schemes, gathering in golden sheaves of wealth from the harvest-fields of trade.

"Am I happier for all this?" he said, questioning with himself; "does the larger increase add to my pleasure? Do houses and lands bring peace of mind, or ships upon the ocean a tranquil spirit? Rather, do not all these things multiply cares? Is my sleep sounder than it was twenty years ago, or my heart lighter?"

Away back into the past went his thoughts, as the last sentence was uttered, and he remembered the time when, with the closing of day, he could dismiss the day's business, and find a pure delight in the humble home where wife and children welcomed his return with gladness. Now his magnificent dwelling was as little enjoyed as a prisoner's cell; for his affections were not there, but winging their way, with his thoughts, afar off, to distant seas or strange lands, or hovering about amid brilliant schemes, golden with the promise of untold wealth.

Algernon sighed as he contrasted days gone by with the present, and his heart acknowledged that he was happier then than now. The merchant was in a softer mood than usual; and it was well for the half-starving women, whose white face looked into his imploringly, that it was so. She had thrown herself, almost desperately, in his way, just as he turned from the crowded thoroughfare into a less frequented street, not far from his luxurious home, and with this appeal—

"If you have children, sir, pity mine!"

"What of your children?" asked the merchant, as he stood still, and looked into the woman's pale, pleading face, down upon which the rays of the gas lamp fell, and showed its lines of sorrow and suffering.

"They are hungry, and I have no food for

them; they are sick, and I cannot get them medicine."

"Is this true?" said the merchant, half in doubt. Such extremity seemed almost impossible to him.

"Come and see! Oh, sir, come and see!" Hope, doubt, anguish, all blended in that mother's voice.

"Where is your home?" asked Algernon.

"Only in the next street," was replied.

"I will go with you. Lead the way."

Hurrying on before with rapid feet went the eager woman; following, with a quicker movement than usual, came the merchant. They were soon at an old pile of buildings, not far from the place of meeting. The woman entered, and Algernon followed. The sight that met his eye stirred all the man within him, and awakened his utmost pity. A sick child, with hollow cheeks, waxen face, and large, glistening eyes, lay upon an old quilt on the floor; another wan-looking child sat crouching in the chimney corner, trying to warm her half-naked body by the almost imperceptible heat of a few dying coals; while a third, not over six years of age, stood on the other side of the fireplace, mumbling at a bone from which it was impossible to extract nutrition.

"It is even so," said the merchant, as he glanced in painful surprise about the room. Then he gave the woman money, and told her to go quickly for food to nourish her children, and fuel to warm them. Nor did humanity end its good work here. He went to a store in the neighborhood, and purchased beds and bed clothing for the destitute family, and saw these comforts conveyed to the room they occupied, and the children, after being warmed and fed, laid in them with their faces full of wonder and gladness.

In a single half-hour Algernon, the merchant, had changed the cold, desolate home of a poor widow into what to her and her children was now a Paradise of comfort. There was a large glowing fire upon the hearth, making the air of the room rosy with light, and genial with warmth. Added to a few broken chairs and an old table, which constituted the only furniture in the apartment, were two plain bedsteads, with beds and warm clothing laid over them, giving their promise of rest and comfort in the long cold nights. Flour, meal, meat, bread, sufficient to supply the little family for weeks, were piled up in one corner, and the mother crumpled tightly in her hands a slip of paper containing an order for fuel enough to last the winter through.

"May He who pities the widow and the fatherless be better to you than this, even a thousand fold!" said the woman, as Algernon was leaving. Her eyes were full of tears, but the heart's warm glow of thankfulness was on her face and in her voice. "And may the memory of this good deed go with you as a blessing through life!"

An hour later, and the merchant sat alone in one of the luxurious apartments of his palace-home. A book lay on the table beside him, and his hand rested upon an open page. He had been reading, and this sentiment had arrested his attention, and given his thoughts a new direction—"We only possess what we have bestowed." At first the strangely-sounding apothegm struck him as a paradox.

"Possess only what we have bestowed!" said he, talking with himself. "How can I possess what I have given to another? The thing is absurd. And yet this writer is not in the habit of uttering absurd things. What does he mean?"

Algernon turned to the book again and read on. "Only what we enjoy do we really possess" He lifted his eyes from the page again, and mused on this other proposition.

"There is truth somewhere here—a newer and higher truth than my thought has yet apprehended," Algernon talked on again with himself. "I have acquired great possessions—are they enjoyed? Am I happier now than when my wealth could be told in half the figures it now takes to record the sum? I have lands, houses, ships, gold, merchandise—do I really possess them—that is, in this sense of enjoyment? Do they not, in fact, weigh heavier upon my spirit with each new accumulation, making possession but a mockery?"

From ships, and merchandise, houses and lands, the thought of Algernon turned to the widow and her children, relieved from suffering under the sudden activity of an impulsive benevolence.

Instantly a glow of pleasure warmed his heart, and a thrill of delight went trembling to the very centre of his being. Thirty dollars had this good deed cost him in money; and already he was in the possession of higher enjoyments therefrom than all his day's large accumulations had given.

"This I possess!" he said, with rising enthusiasm. "This I have for all time, and for all eternity, a source of perennial pleasure. Moth cannot corrupt it, fire cannot burn it, thieves cannot break through and steal it away. I can lay me down in the grave, and yet not lose my hold upon it. Is not this possession in its sublimest sense!"

Then the thoughts of Algernon went back upon his life, turning the pages of memory, and searching for the good deeds he had done. They were "few and far between," but around each was a halo that illumined the whole page. Side by side with the good deeds were recorded the gains of the merchant; but always some other memory shadowed these records of gain, and robbed them blessing.

"These — these," said the merchant, as his thoughts returned to the present, "are my only real possessions. And yet how few they are—how poor I am! Algernon, the rich merchant, has made small accumulations, indeed! But, thanks to the Teacher, he has found the way that leads to another El Dorado."

XVIII.

ENEMIES.

"I know whose work that is," said Mrs. Edwards. "I can trace her hand in every part of it." The speaker's brow grew dark, and her eyes flashed with anger. "She's bound to do me all the harm she can; but I will be even with her."

"Why should Mrs. Grant seek to injure you?" inquired the lady to whom the above remark was addressed.

"Because she is an enemy."

"An enemy?"

"Yes, an enemy. And she is not the only one I have."

"Why should you have enemies, Mrs. Edwards?" asked the lady.

"Why does any one have enemies? Let a man go straight forward through the world—independent, self-reliant, yielding to none, humoring none

—and, my word for it, he will find himself encompassed with a cloud of enemies. People never forgive those who are indifferent to them."

"Indifferent! What do you mean by indifferent? Let me understand you clearly, Mrs. Edwards."

"I make my own world," was answered; "or, at least, make it up of my own, and leave my neighbors to do the same. I concern myself only about my own things, and never give encouragement to meddlers, of whom there are a great abundance. Out of every three persons you meet, two will be found over inquisitive in regard to your affairs. I never gratify them."

"Why?" was the quiet inquiry.

"Because it is none of their business. As, for instance, there is Mrs. Lewis. If I buy a new dress, a piece of lace, or linen, or make any addition to my wardrobe that she happens to discover, straightway leaps out a question as to the price. But she never gets anything out of me."

"How do you manage, in such cases, so as not to give offence?"

"Sometimes I evade the question; sometimes I mislead by giving a price higher or lower than was actually paid; and sometimes I deal in a little sarcasm, that may be taken or not, as the person chooses. But nothing is ever learned of my affairs. What I pay for goods, and where I buy them, is my own affair altogether."

"And your neighbors too, I think, if the knowledge is of service to them, and no loss to you," said the lady with whom Mrs. Edwards was conversing.

"I don't see it so," was firmly answered. "Let people do their own shopping, and find the cheap places and choice patterns for themselves. I'm not disposed to gain knowledge for their advantage."

"Our candle burns none the dimmer for the light it gives to the candle of another."

"Let people strike their own fires, say I," returned Mrs. Edwards. "I have enough to do to take care of my own. This running about to light the candles of people who are too idle or indifferent to keep their own a-blaze, doesn't suit my genius. I'm not one of the over-charitable kind. Mind your own business is my life-precept."

"There need be no running about to light other people's candles," said the lady. "But it should give us pleasure to communicate, when a person asks to profit by our skill, knowledge, or experience, if the information may be given without injury to ourselves."

"It doesn't give me any pleasure," replied Mrs. Edwards, with an expression in her tone and countenance that repelled her acquaintance, who remembered more than one instance in which she had herself very innocently asked questions that were answered with evasion

"Perhaps," she ventured to remark, "if you were to try the experiment a few times, you would find a higher pleasure in it than you imagine."

"I have no wish to make it, whatever. My own way just suits me. I am neither debtor nor creditor to the world. We stand at quits."

"Indeed! Then I don't wonder that you have enemies, and they of the worst kind; having power to do you harm."

"What harm?" The lady's manner struck Mrs. Edwards as involving some deeper meaning than was apparent on the surface.

"Harm to your soul," was answered, in a serious tone of voice.

"Oh!" Mrs. Edwards slightly tossed her head.

"Our real enemies," said the lady, "are within

us. Those who stand upon the outside—men and women who, from evil purpose, seek to do us harm—can only shatter the external a little, but have no power over the real man. They cannot hurt a hair of our head. Selfish feelings alone are our real enemies, for they hurt the soul; marring its beauty, exhausting its strength, deforming its limbs, and changing it from the image of God into a monster. We cannot live the life of heaven here, Mrs. Edwards, upon your exclusive principle—pardon my freedom of speech. God placed us here, that we might ascend to heaven through the way of good deeds, having their inspiration in a loving spirit. If you refuse to let another's candle be lighted at yours—selfishly refuse—the light of God's love will go out in your soul, and leave you in the darkness of eternal night."

The lady arose, and moved a step away from Mrs. Edwards, not doubting that she had given offence, and half regretting that she had been betrayed into such plainness of speech. But the boldness of her positions, the almost solemn manner in which she had spoken, and, withal, her social standing and estimable character—all had the effect to startle, rather than offend Mrs. Edwards.

"You have a strange way of talking," said the latter, rising at the same time, and looking steadily, but without sign of feeling, at her free-spoken monitor.

"I have given utterance only to words of truth, and they have no limited or merely individual application, but involve the laws of heavenly life," was calmly answered. "As I have not meant to offend, I trust you will not take offence. I have spoken to do you good, not evil—as a friend, and not as an enemy."

"I am not quite so bad," said Mrs. Edwards, with signs of feeling, "as my words make me out. I talk a little at random, and perhaps a little in earnest, sometimes. But I thank you for the truth, and honor you for womanly candor. The enemies you have pointed out, I will watch, lest, in an unguarded moment, they do me some fatal injury."

"None others can do us real harm," was gently answered. "Heaven guards us from all outside enemies, or gives us strength to overcome their assaults. Only the secret foes, lurking in our own breasts, can wound us in vital places."

XIX.

DUTY AND KINDNESS.

There was an angry frown on the countenance of Deacon Jonas Browning. There were tears on on the sad face of his wife.

"He shall be sent to sea!" said Deacon Browning, sternly.

There was a pleading look in the eyes of Mrs. Browning, as she lifted them to the iron face of her husband. But no words passed her lips.

"He shall be sent to sea! It is my last hope."

"Philip is very young, Jonas," said Mrs. Browning.

"Not too young for evil, and, therefore, not too young for the discipline needed to eradicate evil. He shall go to sea! Captain Ellis sails in the Fanny Williams on next Monday. I will call upon him this very day."

"Isn't the Fanny Williams a whaler?" The lips

of Mrs. Browning quivered, and her voice had a choking sound.

"Yes," was firmly answered.

"I wouldn't send him away in a whaler, Jonas. Remember—he is very young, not thirteen until next April."

"Young or old, Mary, he's got to go," said the stern deacon, who was a believer in the gospel of law. He was no weak advocate of moral suasion, as it is familiarly termed. He went in for law, and was a strict constructionist. Implicit obedience was the statute for home, and all deviations therefrom met the never withheld penalty.

Mrs. Browning entered into no argument with her husband, for she knew that would be useless. She had never succeeded in changing his purpose by argument in her life. And so she bent her eyes meekly to the floor again, while the tears crept over her face, and fell in large bright drops upon the carpet. Deacon Browning saw the tears, but they did not move him. He was tear-proof.

Philip, the offending member of the Browning family, was a bright, active, restless boy, who, from the start, had been a rebel against unreasonable authority, and, as a matter of course, not unfrequently against authority both just and reasonable. Punishment had only hardened him; increasing, instead of diminishing, his power of endurance. The particular offence for which he was now in disgrace, was, it must be owned, rather a serious one. He had, in company with three other boys of his age, known as the greatest reprobates in the village, rifled a choice plum tree, belonging to a neighbor, of all the fruit it contained, and then killed a favorite dog, which, happening to discover them at their wicked work, attempted to drive them from the garden. The neighbor had complained to Deacon Browning, accompanying his complaint with a threat to have Philip arrested for stealing.

"If you don't do something with that boy of yours," he added with considerable feeling, "he'll end his days in the State Prison, or on the gallows."

Hard words were these for the ears of Deacon Browning, the rigidly righteous! Hard words, and with a prophetic conviction in them. He had not a very creative imagination, but in this instance the prediction of his angry neighbor conjured up in his mind the image of a prison and a gallows, causing a shudder to pass along his nerves, and the cold perspiration to start upon his forehead. From that moment the resolution of Deacon Browning was taken.

The boy was on the brink of ruin, and must be saved at all hazards. As to the means of doing this, it never entered into the heart of Deacon Browning to conceive of any other than such as involved harsh discipline. The Canaanite was in the land and must be driven out with fire and sword. With him the word duty had a stern significance. He had always tried to do his duty, moving steadily onward in the path of life, and crushing down all vanities and evils that sprang up by the way, under a heel shod with iron.

"He shall be sent to sea!" That was the last desperate remedy. In his mind, as in the minds of many like him, some years ago, a ship was the great school of reform; and when a boy was deemed incorrigible, he was sent off to sea, usually to have his evil inclinations hardened into permanent qualities.

When Deacon Browning met his son Philip, after receiving intelligence of his great offence, it was with a stern, angry repulsion. He did not see the look of appeal, the sign of repentance, the plea for mercy, that was in his tearful eyes. A single word of kindness would have broken up the great deep of the boy's heart, and impelled by the warmer impulses inherited from his mother, he would have flung himself, weeping, into his father's arms. But Deacon Browning had separated duty from kindness. The one was a stern corrector of evil, the other a smiling approver of good.

From his home to the wharf, where the Fanny Williams lay, all equipped for sea, Deacon Browning bent his steps. Captain Ellis, a rough, hard man, was on board. After listening to the father's story and request, he said, bluntly—

"If you put your boy on board the Fanny Williams, he'll have to bend or break, that's certain. Take my advice, and give the matter a second thought. He'll have a dog's life of it in a whaler. It's my opinion that your lad hasn't stuff enough in him for this experiment."

"I'll risk it," replied the Deacon. "He's got too much stuff in him to stay at home, that's the trouble. The bend or break system is the only one in which I have any faith."

"As you like, Deacon. I want another boy, and yours will answer, I guess."

"When do you sail?" was inquired.

"On Monday."

"Very well. I'll bring the boy down to-morrow."

The thing was settled; the Deacon did not feel altogether comfortable in mind. Philip was young for such an experiment, as the mother had urged. And now very opportunely, a leaf in the book of his memory was turned, on which was written the story of a poor boy's wrongs and sufferings at sea. Many years before, his heart had grown sick over the record. He tried to look away from the page, but could not. It seemed to hold his eye by a kind of fascination.

Still he did not relent. Duty required him to go steadily forward and execute his purpose. There was no other hope for the boy.

"Philip!" It was thus that he announced his determination. "I am going to send you to sea with Captain Ellis. It's my last hope. Steadily bent, as you are, on evil, I can no longer suffer you to remain at home. The boy who begins with robbing his neighbor's garden, is in great danger of ending his career upon the gallows. To save you, if possible, from a fate like this, I now send you to sea."

Very sternly, very harshly, almost angrily, was this said. Not the smallest impression did it seem to make upon the boy, who stood with his eyes cast down, an image of stubborn self-will and persistent rebellion.

With still sharper denunciation did the father speak, striving in this way to shock the feelings of his child, and extort signs of penitence. But it was the hammer and the anvil—blow and rebound.

Very different were the mother's efforts with the child. Tearfully she pleaded with him—earnestly she besought him to ask his father's forgiveness for the evil he had done. But Philip said—

"No, mother. I would rather go to sea. Father don't love me—he don't care for me. He hates me, I believe."

"Philip! Philip! Don't speak in that way of your father. He does love you; and it is only for your good that he is going to send you to sea. Oh, how could you do so wicked a thing?"

Tears were in the mother's eyes. But the boy had something of the father's stern spirit in him, and showed no weakness.

"It isn't any worse than he did when he was a boy," was his answer.

"Philip!"

"Well, it isn't; for I heard Mr. Wright tell Mr. Freeman that father and he robbed orchards and hens' nests; and did worse than that, when they were boys!"

Poor Mrs. Browning was silent. Well did she remember how wild a boy Jonas Browning was; and how, when she was a little girl, she had heard all manner of evil laid to his charge.

Very unexpectedly—at least to Mr. Browning—the minister called in on the evening of that troubled day. After some general conversation with the family, he asked to have a few words with the deacon alone.

"Is it true, Mr. Browning," he said, after they had retired to an adjoining room, "that you are going to send Philip to sea?"

"Too true," replied the father, soberly. "It is my last hope. From the beginning that boy has been a rebel against just authority; and though I have never relaxed discipline, through the weakness of natural feelings, yet resistance has grown with his growth and strengthened with his strength, until duty requires me to use a desperate remedy for a desperate disease. It is a painful trial; but the path of duty is the only path of safety. What we see to be right, we must execute with unflinching courage. I cannot look back and accuse myself of any neglect of duty towards this boy, through weakness of the flesh. From the beginning, I have made obedience the law of my household, and suffered no deviation therefrom to go unpunished."

"Duty," said the minister, "has a twin sister."

He spoke in a changed voice, and with a manner that arrested the attention of Deacon Browning, who looked at him with a glance of inquiry.

"She is as lovely and gentle, as he is hard and unyielding."

The deacon still looked curious.

"When the twin sister of duty is away from his side, he loses more than half of his influence; but, in her beautiful presence, he gains a dignity and power that make his precepts laws of life to all who hear them. The stubborn heart melts, the iron will is subdued; the spirit of evil shrinks away from the human soul."

There was a pause.

"The name of that twin sister is Kindness."

The eyes of Deacon Browning fell away from

the minister's countenance, and drooped until they rested upon the floor. Conviction flashed upon his heart. He had always been stern in executing the law—but never kind?

"Has that beautiful twin sister stood ever by the side of Duty?—has love been in the law, Deacon Browning?"

Side by side with the minister stood Duty and Kindness—the firm, unshrinking brother, and the mild, loving sister—and so his word had power to reach the deacon's heart, without giving offence to pride.

"Kindness is weak, yielding, and indulgent, and forgives when punishment is the only hope of salvation," said Deacon Browning, a little recovering himself from the first emotions of self-condemnation.

"Only when she strays from the side of Duty," replied the minister. "Duty and Kindness must always act together."

Much more, and to the same purpose, was urged by the minister, who made only a brief visit, and then withdrew, that his admonitions might work the effect desired.

When Deacon Browning came in from the front

door of his house, after parting with the minister, he drew a chair up to the table in the family sitting-room, and, almost involuntarily, opened the large family Bible. His feelings were much softened towards his boy, who, with his head bowed upon his breast, sat a little apart from his mother. The attitude was not so much indicative of stubborn self-will, as suffering. Deacon Browning thought he would read a chapter aloud, and so drew the holy book closer, and bent his face down over it. Mrs. Browning, observing the movement, waited for him to begin. The deacon cleared his throat twice. But his voice did not take up the words that were in his eyes and in his heart. How could they?

"As a father pitieth his children"——

Had there been divine pity in the heart of Deacon Browning for his rebellious and unhappy boy? Nay—had there not been wrath, instead?

"As a father *pitieth* his children"——

From a hundred places in the mind of Deacon Browning there seemed to come an echo of these words, and they had a meaning in them never perceived before. He closed the book, and remained in deep thought for many minutes; and not only in deep thought, but in a stern conflict with himself. Kindness was striving to gain her place by the side of Duty; and cold, hard, imperious Duty, who had so long ruled without a rival in the mind of Deacon Browning, kept all the while averting his countenance from that of his twin sister, who had been so long an exiled wanderer. At last she was successful. The stern brother yielded, and clasped to his bosom the sister who sought his love.

From that instant new thoughts, new views, new purposes ruled in the mind of Deacon Browning. The discipline of a whaler was too hard and cruel for his boy, young in years, and by no means as hardened in iniquity as he had permitted himself to imagine. A cold shiver ran along his nerves at the bare thought of doing what, a few hours before, he had so resolutely intended. Kindness began whispering in the ears of Duty, and crowding them with a world of new suggestions. The heart of the stern man was softened, and there flowed into it something of a mother's yearning tenderness. Rising up, at length, Deacon Browning said, in a low voice, so new in its tones to the ears of Philip, that it made his heart leap—

"My son, I wish to see you alone."

The deacon went into the next room, and Philip followed him. The deacon sat down, and Philip stood before him.

"Philip, my son"—Deacon Browning took the boy's hand in one of his, and looked him full in the face. The look was returned—not a defiant look, but one of yielding wonder.

"Philip, I am not going to send you to sea with Captain Ellis. I intended doing so; but, on reflection, I think the life will be too hard for you."

Very firmly, yet kindly, the deacon tried to speak, but the sister of Duty was playing with his heart-strings, and their tone of pity was echoed from his voice, that faltered when he strove to give it firmness.

The eyes of Philip remained fixed upon the countenance of his father.

"My son"— Deacon Browning thought he had gained sufficient self-control to utter calmly certain mild forms of admonition; but he was in error; his voice was still less under his control, and so fully betrayed the new-born pity and tenderness in his heart, that Philip, melting into penitence, exclaimed, as tears, gushed from his eyes—

"Oh, father! I've been very wicked, and very sorry!"

Involuntarily, at this unexpected confession, the arms of Deacon Browning were stretched out towards his repentant boy, and Philip rushed, sobbing, into them.

The boy was saved. From that hour his father had him under the most perfect subordination. But the twin sister of Duty walked ever by his side.

XX.

IMPERISHABLE BEAUTY.

It was a very plain face. My eye rested upon it, for a moment or two, and then wandered away to the countenance of another maiden, whose beauty ravished the eyes of every beholder; and as I gazed with a feeling of delight, upon its transcendent loveliness, an impulse of thankfulness stirred in my heart—thankfulness to the Creator of beauty. The first maiden sat alone; around the other stood a group of admirers. So marked a contrast between the two, as well in features as in the impression made thereby, excited, first, something like pity for her whom nature had endowed so poorly; and I turned to look at her again with a kinder feeling in my heart.

There she sat all alone. Yes, her face was very, very plain; but it did not strike me as repulsive. The mouth, which had nothing of the ripe fullness that gave such an enamoring grace to the other maiden, was placid; and though not encircled by a perpetual wreath of smiles, calmly enthroned the gentle spirit of content. Her eyes were small, the lashes thin, and the arch above them faintly visible. Arch? I can scarcely give it that graceful designation. I had not yet seen the expression of those eyes. As I looked towards her, with that strange consciousness of observation which all have remarked, but which few can explain, she turned her eyes from another part of the room, and looked at me. They did not flash brilliantly, nor strike me, at the first glance, as having in them anything peculiar. They were the common eyes we meet at every turn—no soul in them. I give my first impression. My second was different. I had turned my eyes away; but something I had seen, caused them almost involuntarily to wander back to the maiden's face. A friend whom I highly regarded—a young man of more than common worth—had crossed the room, and was standing before her. She had lifted her eyes to his face, and there was a new light in them—not a dazzling, but a soft, winning light, that purity and love made almost beautiful.

They were conversing, and I watched, for some time, the play of that unattractive countenance—unattractive no longer.

"Ah!" said I, "there is a beautiful soul within that casket."

And as I spoke thus, in the silence of my own thoughts, I looked towards the other maiden, who was still surrounded by a crowd of admirers.

"Her beauty is wonderful!" I could not help the utterance of this tribute to her charms. Yet scarcely had I spoken the words, when she turned to one of the group which had gathered about her, a slight curl of unlovely scorn upon her lips, and threw at him an arrowy word that wounded as it struck. She saw that it hurt, and a gleam of pleasure went forth from her brilliant eyes.

A filmy veil came between me and that countenance, which, a little while before, had shone with a loveliness that was absolutely enchanting. I turned again to the other maiden. My friend still stood before her, and her eyes were lifted to his face. She was uttering some sentiments—what, I did not hear—but they must have been good and beautiful in conception, to have filled every lineament with such a winning grace.

"Ah!" said I, the real truth dawning upon my mind, "here is the inner, imperishable beauty. The beauty, which, instead of losing its spring-time freshness, forever advances towards eternal youth."

A few weeks later, and my friend communicated to me the intelligence, that his heart had been won by the charms of this unattractive maiden. Once he had been a worshipper at the other shrine—the shrine of beauty; and I knew that, only a few months before, hand and heart were ready to be offered. Accepted they would have been, for he had personal beauty, attractive manners, wealth, and above all, a manly, honorable spirit.

For all I had seen, I was scarcely prepared for this. The maiden might be good—I did not question that—but she was so homely; and this homeliness would be only the more apparent in contrast with his elegant exterior. It was almost on my lip to remonstrate—to suggest this thought to his mind. But I prudently forbore.

"You know her well, I hope." I could not help the utterance of this caution.

"She is not thought to be beautiful," he replied, seeming to perceive my thoughts, "indeed, as to features, she is plain; yet, in person, she is tall, graceful, dignified, and with a carriage that a queen might envy."

This was true to the letter. I had not thought of it before. Nature had given at least this compensation.

"But the higher beauty," he added, "is of the soul. All else is soon diminished. Scarcely has the blushing girl stepped forward through the opening door of womanhood, ere we see the lustre of her blossoming cheek beginning to tarnish in the social atmosphere, or to pale from disease. But the soul's beauty dims not, wanes not, dies not. It is as imperishable as the soul itself. Our bodies die, but the soul is immortal."

"If she possesses this beauty?"

"I know that she possesses it," he answered, warmly. "I have seen it looking forth from her eyes, wreathing about her lips, and giving to every lineament a heavenly charm. It is musical in every tone of her voice."

"Goodness alone is beautiful," I said.

"And she is good," he replied. "I never met one who so rarely spoke of herself, or who seemed to take so loving an interest in humanity."

"That is God-like."

"Is not God the very source of all beauty? To be God-like, then, is to be beautiful. Ah!" he added, "I have found, indeed, a treasure! Morning and evening I thank the good Giver, that he opened my eyes to see deeper than the unalluring surface. I was dazzled, once, by a glittering exterior; but have a clearer vision now."

"Win her and wear her, then," I replied, "and may she be to you all your fancy pictures."

"She is won," he answered, "and I shall wear her proudly in the eyes of all men."

There was a world of surprise when it became known that my handsome friend was about leading his chosen bride to the marriage altar.

"How could he throw himself away upon such an ugly creature?" said one, coarsely.

"He might have taken his choice from the loveliest," remarked another.

"He will tire of that face in a month. All the gold of Ophir would not bribe me to sit opposite to it for a year."

And so the changes rung.

But my friend knew what he was doing. I was present at the wedding.

"If she were not so homely!" I heard a lady remark, as she stood beside her handsome young husband. "What can he see in her to love?"

I turned and looked at the speaker. Nature had been kind in giving her an attractive face; but the slight curl of contempt that was on her lip marred everything. I glanced back to the young bride's countenance; her pure soul was shining through it, like light through a veil. To me, she seemed at that moment more beautiful than the other; and far more worthy to be loved.

The brilliantly beautiful maiden of whom I have spoken, gave her hand in marriage about the same time. Her husband was a young man of good character, kind feelings, and with sufficient income to enable them to live in a style of imposing elegance. A series of gay parties was the social welcome given to the lovely bride. But such honor did not attend the nuptials of her plainer sister.

A few years later, and the spiritual qualities of each were more apparent in their faces. I remember meeting both, in company, ten years after their marriage. I was standing at one end of the room, when an over-dressed woman, with a showy face, came in, accompanied by a gentleman whom I knew, not as an acquaintance, but as a man of business and the husband of the beauty. I should scarcely have recognized the latter, but for him. What a change was there! At a distance, the face struck you as still beautiful, but, on a closer view, the illusion vanished. The mouth had grown sensual, peevish, and ill-natured; the eyes were bright, but the brightness repelled rather than attracted. After awhile, wondering at the change, I drew near and entered into conversation with her. The music of her voice I remembered. There was no music in it now; at least none for my ears. A certain abruptness in her manners, born of pride, or superciliousness, was to me particularly offensive. I tried her on various subjects, in order to bring out some better aspects of her character. The Swedish Nightingale had just been here, and had sung to my heart as no living man or woman had ever sung—I spoke of her. "Too artificial," was the reply, with an air of critical vanity, that gave to my feelings a ripple of indignation. I referred to a new poem, admirable for its purity of style; she coldly remarked with depreciation on some of its special beauties, merely repeating, as I knew, a certain captious reviewer. I was in doubt whether she had read even a page of the book. Then I spoke of a lady present. She tossed her head, and arched her lip, saying, "She's too fond of gentlemen's attentions."

I varied still my efforts, but to no good purpose. The more I conversed with her, the less beautiful became her face, for the unloveliness of her true character was perpetually gleaming through and spoiling the already sadly-marred features. I left her side, on the first good opportunity, glad to get away. Ten years ago, in all companies, she was the cynosure of every eye. The praise of her beauty was on every lip. But so changed was she now, that none bent to do her reverence. I noticed her sitting alone, with a discontented look, long after I had left my place by her side. Her husband, for all the attentions he paid her during the evening, might have been unconscious of her presence.

But there was another lady in the room, who was, all the while, the centre of an admiring circle. None, perhaps, considered her face beautiful; yet to every one who looked upon it, came a perception of beauty that associated itself with her individuality. In repose, her features were plain, yet not repulsive in the slightest particular. But, when thought and feeling flowed into them, every eye was charmed. There was a nameless grace in her manner that gave additional power to the attractions of her countenance.

I was half in doubt, at first, of her identity, as I gazed upon her from a distant part of the room; she looked, in my eyes, so really beautiful. But the presence of my old friend in the group, my old friend who had been wise enough to prefer beauty of soul to beauty of face, removed all questions, and passing over, I added another to the circle which had gathered around her.

There was nothing obtrusive in her conversation; nothing of conscious pride; but a calm, and, at times, earnest utterance of true sentiments. Not once during the evening did I hear a word from her lips that jarred the better feelings.

"The good are beautiful!" Many times did this sentiment find spontaneous utterance in my thoughts as I looked upon her; and then turned my eyes to the discontented face of another, who, a few years before, carried off, in every company, the palm of loveliness.

Yes, here was the imperishable beauty! Maiden!

would you find this beauty? No matter if your features were not cast in classic mould, this higher, truer beauty may be yours if you will seek for it in the denial of selfishness, and the repression of discontent. "The good are beautiful." Lay that up in your thoughts. Treasure it as the most sublime wisdom.

Gather into the store-house of your minds sentiments of regard for others; and let your hands engage in gentle charities. To do good and to communicate forget not. If tempted to murmur, think of your many blessings; if to repine, of the thousands who are sick and in suffering. Be humble, gentle, forgiving, and above all—useful. These are the graces that shine through the outer coverings of the soul, and reveal themselves in light and loveliness to all eyes.

The good never grow homely as they grow old. The outer eye may become dim, and the cheek loose its freshness, but in the place of earthly charms will come a spiritual beauty, unfading as eternity.

XXI.

NEIGHBOR GRAY.

"HAVE you met our new neighbor Gray, friend Tompkins?" inquired one farmer of another. They were at Peter Craig's blacksmith shop.

"No; and what's more, I don't want to meet him," was abruptly answered.

"Don't want to meet him?"

"No! I've said just what I mean," replied Tompkins, ill-naturedly. "I don't want to meet him, nor have anything to do with him."

"You'll change your mind, I think," said the blacksmith.

"Will I?" A sneer curled the lip of farmer Tompkins.

"Yes, and that before Mr. Gray is two months in Splinterville," replied Peter Craig. "But, pray, tell us what you have against our new neighbor.

"Oh, nothing very particular, only I don't like him."

"There is one thing to be said in his favor," remarked the blacksmith—"he keeps good stock."

"Humph! No better than is to be found in the neighborhood," said Tompkins. "No better, in fact, than I have."

"I'm not so sure of that," returned Peter Craig. "I put shoes on his carriage horses yesterday, and, if I'm any judge, their match is not within ten miles of these parts. No, no, friend Tompkins, you hav'n't the horseflesh on your sixty acres that will compare with neighbor Gray's.

"Bah! neighbor Gray's! Nobody's got anything, from a patent pitchfork up to a threshing machine, that will compare with neighbor Gray's! It makes me downright angry to hear people talk after this fashion. Who's Mr. Gray, I'd like to know?"

"He's a gentleman," said the blacksmith, a little warmly.

"Gentleman!" Tompkins spoke with a bitter sneer, "I hate gentlemen!"

"The gentleman is the only true man," remarked Peter Craig.

"Of course: kid gloves, calf-skin, broadcloth, and beaver, are everything, and the individual nothing."

"Not so fast, friend Tompkins; not so fast. It is the heart that makes the gentleman."

"If that is the case, I don't think there's much chance for your new neighbor. But, gentleman, or no gentleman, I detest this Gray from the bottom of my heart, and wish he were a thousand miles away from Splinterville!"

As Tompkins closed this sentence, in a pretty loud tone of voice, his ear caught the sound of a footstep, and turning quickly, he saw Mr. Gray approaching through the blacksmith's shop, having entered by the opposite door from the one near which the little group of men were standing. He was near enough to have heard the closing sentence, and, from the expression of his countenance, it was pretty evident that its meaning was understood.

The moment Tompkins saw him, his face crimsoned, and, turning off abruptly, he strode away. As he did so, he thought he heard the voice of Mr. Gray calling after him. But he had not the manliness to stop and meet, face to face, the individual whose name he had used so freely.

An ill-natured, jealous-minded, unhappy kind of a man was this Tompkins. You will find his counterpart in almost every neighborhood. Mr. Gray, towards whom he cherished such unkind feelings, had bought, some months before, the farm that immediately adjoined his, and, a few weeks previously, taken formal possession. Now, Tompkins wanted this farm, and had been for some time endeavoring to strike a bargain with its previous owner, when Mr. Gray, seeing the property advertised for sale, complied with the terms, and became the purchaser. Tompkins wished to exchange his farm for the other, and give notes for the difference in price; and although the owner had two or three times declined his offer, he was still in hope of making the arrangement, when Mr. Gray dashed all his hopes to the ground.

From that moment he hated Mr. Gray in his heart, and wished him all manner of evil. But for all this, Tompkins didn't feel very comfortable in mind about the harsh sentence which he was very certain Mr. Gray had heard. Talk as freely as he would behind his neighbor's back, he was not quite prepared to denounce him to his face; and for this reason, if for none other, he could show no cause for his animosity. The farm was in market, and his new neighbor had as good a right to purchase as any one else. It was not at all probable that Mr. Gray knew anything about his previous negotiations; and even if he had, that was no reason why he should not purchase if an offer of the farm were made to him.

Compelled now to look at the affair as if looking upon it with other people's eyes, Tompkins was not able to justify himself in the unkind attitude he had taken. Imagination brought him face to face with the incensed Mr. Gray, who said to him, in a stern, demanding voice:

"What is the meaning of this language? What have I done, that you detest me, and wish me a thousand miles away from Splinterville?"

In vain did farmer Tompkins seek to frame some reply in his thoughts that would have the appearance of justification. It would not answer to refuse giving any reason for his conduct; for that would place him in the light of a mere traducer of his neighbor without cause. Nor would it do to state the true reason; for that was one which, however valid in his own eyes, could hardly appear so in the eyes of anybody else.

Farmer Tompkins was in something of a quandary. He had brought himself into rather a humiliating relation to this new neighbor; and the more he thought about it, the less clearly did he see himself honorably out of his trouble.

But Tompkins was not the man to "humble himself," to use his own words, to any one, by acknowledging that he had done wrong, no matter how sharp were his own convictions on the subject. And of all men in the world, Mr. Gray was the last to whom he would make humiliating acknowledgments. He hated and despised him the more now that he felt himself something in his power. And he determined to brave it out. If neighbor Gray called upon him for explanations, he would insult him to his face!

On the next morning Tompkins had occasion to visit the blacksmith's shop again.

"What did that Gray have to say about me yesterday?" he asked of Peter Craig, in his most abrupt, ill-natured manner.

"He didn't mention your name," replied the blacksmith.

The farmer looked surprised.

"He must have heard me."

"I rather think he did," said the blacksmith.

"And didn't say anything at all?"

"Not about you."

Farmer Tompkins was puzzled and disappointed. Much as he hated, and affected to despise Mr. Gray, he felt nervous about the effect produced upon him by the harsh words he had spoken; and he had hoped to get some clue thereto from the blacksmith.

A few hours later in the day, as he was riding away from home, he saw his new neighbor approaching along the road not far distant. Obeying the first impulse of his mind, he turned his horse's head, and struck off into a narrow lane, that took him nearly a mile out of his way. In consequence, he was too late for an appointment at which some important business was to be done, and lost an expected advantage.

"I wish this Gray had been in the Dead Sea before he thought of coming to Splinterville," was his angry ejaculation, when, on arriving at the appointed place, he found the business closed, and all the benefit he had hoped to gain forever beyond his reach.

Just as farmer Tompkins, on returning from his fruitless ride, came in sight of home, he saw Mr. Gray leaving the house. He rubbed his eyes, and looked again. Yes; it was even so. Mr. Gray was passing through the gate; and now was moving down the road in the direction of his own home. Tompkins slackened the speed of his horse so that he might not come too fully in view until Mr. Gray reached a bend in the road, around which he passed out of sight.

"What did that fellow want?" he asked, sharply, of his wife, on reaching home.

"Of whom are you speaking?" she inquired.

"Why of Gray; confound him!"

"He merely asked for you," replied the wife.

"Did he say that he would call again?"

"No."

"Humph!" Farmer Tompkins was worried. It was plain that Mr. Gray was not a man to be assailed and traduced without calling his traducer to an account. So far as vituperation was concerned, farmer Tompkins found that an easy matter—it came as "natural as eating." But the thought of being called to an account—of being asked for explanations—of being required to give reasons for the strong language he had seen proper to use, was very far from being agreeable.

All that afternoon, farmer Tompkins was in hourly dread of another call from his new neighbor Gray. Every sound of approaching feet, or sudden call, or noise of the shutting gate, caused him to start, or look up from his work. He was provoked with himself for all this; but, for his life, could not help it. A little while before sundown he came over from the barn to get something from the house. As he came in at the back door, a young woman, wearing a blue sun-bonnet, went out at the front door.

"Who is that?" he asked of his wife.

"Neighbor Gray's girl," was replied.

The farmer's heart gave a quicker bound.

"What did she want?"

He knit his brows as he awaited the answer.

"Mrs. Gray sent over a tumbler of calf's foot jelly for Maggy."

Now, Maggy was a dear little two years' old pet, with soft blue eyes, and light brown hair that fell in wavy circles about her neck, and a heart as full of love, as that of her father was of ill-will to al most every one but herself. To him she was sunlight and joy. The love that gushed forth for her, seemed all the stronger because it had free course in no other direction. But Maggy was sick. A fall fever had seized upon her delicate frame, and wasted her almost to a shadow, and now, although the destroyer had departed from their dwelling, the child was as weak as in the days of earliest infancy.

"Mrs. Gray sent over a tumbler of calf's foot jelly for Maggy."

What an unexpected answer! Farmer Tompkins was altogether unprepared for it.

"How did she know that Maggy was sick?"

His voice was less imperative.

"Mr. Gray asked about her when he was here this morning."

"Who? What?"

Farmer Tompkins was again taken by surprise.

"Mr. Gray asked kindly about her; and when I told him that she was better, looked very much pleased."

The farmer turned his face partly away, so that his wife should not see its expression.

"How does Maggy seem this afternoon?" he asked, a few moments afterwards.

"Better," said the wife.

"I must look at her for a moment; dear little pet!" And Tompkins went into the bedroom where she lay. An older sister stood by her side, holding the calf's foot jelly, and feeding her with it.

"How is my little Maggy?" said the father, as he bent over and kissed her.

"I'm better," she answered, smiling—then added, in a pleased way,

"Don't you think Mrs. Gray was very good to send me this nice calf's foot jelly?"

"Yes, dear."

How could he help answering yes?

When farmer Tompkins returned to the barn, he felt very strangely. There was a pressure on his feelings, for which he could not clearly account; and no wonder—for the farmer was not much given to the observation of his own mental processes. That little act of kindness towards Maggy, so altogether unexpected, had thrown his mind into sudden confusion. He had felt a dislike for Mrs. Gray, simply because he hated her husband—but how could he continue to cherish this feeling for one who had shown kindness towards his little Maggy? It was next to impossible. And Mr.

Gray had asked after Maggy! And further still—it was natural to conclude, that the kind act of his wife had some sort of dependence upon his direction of her thoughts towards the sick child.

"I wish I hadn't said anything against him at Peter Craig's." Now that thought marked the beginning of a better state of mind in farmer Tompkins. "I don't like him; and will never forgive him as long as I live. But there is no occasion to make an enemy even of a dog. And, of course, he's my sworn enemy from this day forth. I wonder what brought him over here. No, I don't wonder either! Well, let him do his worst; he'll find no backing down in Ephraim Tompkins."

On the next morning, Tompkins went over to the blacksmith's shop to see if Peter Craig had finished mending a plough which he had left there some days before. He had said nothing about being in a hurry; and did not really want the plough for a week. But he thought he would step over and see how the work was progressing. As he entered the shop, he saw the plough lying near the forge. But the blacksmith was hammering away upon a wagon tire. Now, although Tompkins didn't want the plough for some days, he felt displeased at seeing his work put aside for the work of somebody else, and said, a little tartly—

"I expected to see that plough finished by this time."

"And so it would have been, friend Tompkins; but our new neighbor, Mr. Gray, had the misfortune to break a wagon-tire yesterday afternoon, just in the midst of some hauling that must be finished by to-morrow. So I let your plough lie, as I knew you were not in a hurry, and was sure you would be willing to oblige Mr. Gray. I will have it all ready for you in the morning."

"To-morrow morning won't do!" said Tompkins, angrily. "I want my plough to-day!"

"I'm sorry," said the blacksmith, in a troubled manner. "I didn't think it would make any difference, or I wouldn't have put aside your work for Mr. Gray or anybody else."

"Oh yes you would!" retorted Tompkins, in a spiteful tone. "Mr. Gray is everything in Splinterville now—and I'm nobody!"

"Don't say that, friend Tompkins," said the blacksmith; "I would do your work as quickly as I would Mr. Gray's. If the plough had belonged to him, and you had come with the broken wagon-tire, I would have laid aside the plough to mend the tire."

But farmer Tompkins was not disposed to listen to reason. This act of letting his work lie over for a day, in order to do that of his neighbor, against whom he had so deep a grudge, made him almost blind with passion, and he was talking in a loud, angry voice, when neighbor Gray's form darkened the door of the blacksmith shop. The new neighbor had called over to see how the mending of the wagon-tire progressed. Just as he entered, Tompkins used his name in connection with some pretty harsh language. Not seeming to notice this, Mr. Gray came forward, and offering his hand to Mr. Tompkins, said very kindly—

"How is your little daughter this morning? I hope she is very much better?"

"She is better, I thank you," replied Tompkins, almost stammering out the words, at the same time that he allowed Mr. Gray to take his hand and shake it, pretty much as he would have shaken a stick.

"I hope," continued Mr. Gray, "that our friend the blacksmith hasn't done anything wrong in laying aside your work to do mine. If so, I pray you to let all the blame fall upon my shoulders. We were so unfortunate as to break our wagon-tire, and all our work was at a stand-still until it was mended. It was one of those emergencies in which all neighbors are ready to accommodate each other, even at the cost of a little inconvenience."

Now, farmer Tompkins hardly expected a greeting like this, and was considerably thrown aback, as the sailors say. The kind inquiry after Maggy —the remembrance of Mrs. Gray's thoughtful attention to the sick child—and, more particularly, the open, frank, friendly manner in which Mr. Gray spoke, all had the effect to disarm him. He wanted to repel the new neighbor—to speak out "his mind" to him—to let him see something of the antagonism that was in his heart. But the cordial good nature, and kind, gentlemanly bearing of Mr. Gray were too much for him, and thawed the ice of his feelings faster than a determined ill nature could freeze the surface.

"I called over yesterday afternoon," continued Mr. Gray, "to mention what I had done; and ask if it would put you to any inconvenience. And I intended to speak with you about a matter which I will mention now. It is this:"

And he drew farmer Tompkins aside, in order that he might talk with him alone.

"I find," he continued, "in having the searches made for the purpose of fixing a true title to the farm just bought, and which adjoins yours, that there has been a clear mistake in running the boundary between your farm and mine—a mistake that includes at least five acres of that fine meadow land to the west of your barn."

"I don't believe a word of it!" exclaimed farmer Tompkins, firing up, and looking the picture of angry indignation. "My title-deeds call for sixty acres, and sixty acres I mean to hold, if I law for it until doomsday!"

"Gently, gently, neighbor Tompkins," replied Mr. Gray. "There need be no trouble about the matter. We don't need any law to settle a business like this. A compromise, where both parties desire to do right, is the easiest thing in the world. You will find me very reasonable."

"It's more than you will find me, then, Mr. Gray, if you attempt to get five acres of my meadow land. I can tell you that, in the beginning."

"I don't want a foot of your land," said Mr. Gray.

"What then do you want?" demanded the exasperated farmer.

"Simply to do right," was the calm reply. "I find that I am considerably over on your line, and that the amount of land I inclose which really belongs to you, is about five acres."

Farmer Tompkins started, looked confused, and flushed to a deeper crimson.

"I requested," continued Mr. Gray, "my conveyancer to go carefully over the matter again, and make his report, which was done yesterday. He says there is no doubt about the matter. I am over the line considerably. Now, what I wish to say is this: I will buy these five acres at a hundred dollars an acre, if you are inclined to sell; if not, I will have my fence removed to the true line, which a surveyor can determine."

We need hardly say that Tompkins was completely disarmed. If a thunderbolt had fallen at his feet he could not have been more surprised. A moment or two he stood in bewilderment of mind; then reaching out his hand to Mr. Gray, he said:

"I am rebuked. Have it your own way. Let the fence stand where it is, and keep the land if you choose—I shall still be as well off as I thought myself an hour ago."

"Right is right, friend Tompkins," replied Mr. Gray. "So if you will walk over to my house, we will settle this business at once. I prefer keeping the land and paying for it the price mentioned."

"It is yours at any price," answered Mr. Tompkins. After a few moments of silence, he added: "I was your enemy, Mr. Gray—your enemy, I now see, without a cause. You have disarmed me in the first encounter. Let us now be friends."

And he reached forth his hand, which was warmly grasped by the new neighbor.

After that, farmer Tompkins was a different man. Mr. Gray proved a true friend, for, both by example and precept, he taught him a better and happier way in the world, and he walked therein with a more cheerful spirit than of old

XXII.

SPIRITUAL PRIDE.

Respectable, orderly, well-to-do-in-the-world people, who have comfortable and, in most cases, eligible pews in church; who are on familiar terms with the minister, and whose opinions, on matters ecclesiastical as well as secular, have weight, are very much inclined to lapse into the impression that they are elevated above the masses of the people in spiritual as well as in external things; that they are better than the poor, the humble, and depressed. You will see them passing up the aisles of our churches, and taking the uppermost seats, with the air of persons whose right to these places are as natural as their right to the elegant homes their money has purchased. And no one questions their right to these seats; for they have a property in them, by honorable purchase, the same as they have in their stores or dwellings.

We are looking below all this, to the spirit that animates them—to the approving self-consciousness which gives quality to the soul.

These individuals are very much in danger of falling into a low kind of spiritual pride. There is a spiritual pride which has its origin in superior intellectual qualities. Because a man is able to talk on theological subjects with some acuteness, and to rise quite above the ordinary range of thought in matters of doctrine, he may indulge the conceit that he is spiritually in advance of his brethren, when he may not have overcome a single evil of his selfish nature. The danger here is very great. But there is another and meaner kind of spiritual pride, which builds its foundation walls on the sandy basis of wealth and mere social rank. The churches are full of this. It is the moth and rust that are eating daily at their inner life. There is a certain fashion in religion, or rather in church-going, which claims of its votaries as nice an observance as is demanded by fashion in dress; and it is far more hurtful than the latter, because it involves a degradation of spiritual things, and makes of the votary, so far as religion is concerned, a mere pretender.

Mrs. Hartman, the wife of a substantial merchant, was very much inclined to indulge in this latter species of spiritual pride, if we may dignify it with the name of "spiritual." She was a pious woman in externals. Her place was never vacant in church, and her demeanor while there was always devout. She never absented herself from the communion table, nor neglected any of the public charities sanctioned by Christian usage. The minister's wife was her very dear friend, and the minister himself a regular visitor at the house. In a general way, Mrs. Hartman talked well on religious themes, which she always made prominent when in the minister's company.

Very naturally did Mrs. Hartman come to think well of herself, in a Christian point of view; and if on some occasions her thoughts could have been seen, they would not have differed very much from those of the Pharisee, so strongly placed by our Lord in contrast with the humble Publican. It is very certain that her estimate of the spiritual condition of the poor people who attended worship in the same church, on each recurring Sabbath, was on a level with her estimate of their natural condition. The external, in her thought, corresponded with the internal; and so she held herself in stately attitudes when she met any of them that she happened to know, or spoke with forced smiles, condescendingly. Some were pleased with her notice; some felt her manner as a spur to pride, and experienced annoyance; while a few met her with quiet, self-possessed exteriors, that a little chafed her in return. Among the latter was a Mrs. Royal, a widow in poor health and poor circumstances. She had two little girls, aged seven and nine years, delicate, sensitive creatures, that were loved by her with a tenderness that grew deeper as health and strength declined. By her needle she earned the bread that nourished them. At one time she had sewing from the family of Mrs. Hartman; but she did not seem grateful enough for the privilege of making up the under-garments of Mrs. Hartman's children; and once was so thoughtless as to say, in a moment of earnest expression on some religious theme, "Sister Hartman."

Sister Hartman! Humph! she is getting past herself." Thus the lady soliloquized, after the poor sewing woman had withdrawn. "I shall have her calling, and leaving her card, as the next move. She doesn't know her place, and never did. She's quite too familiar. Her way of speaking to me on Sundays, if we happen to meet in the vestibule, has always annoyed me. I shall send her no more work."

And Mrs. Hartman kept her word. Mrs. Royal never called, however, to leave her card, as the other had affected to apprehend. But if she happened to meet her anywhere, it was with the old quiet, self-possessed exterior, that Mrs. Hartman's pride of position felt almost as an insult.

It so happened, in the progress of benevolent movements connected with the church, that the formation of a home for orphan children was projected. The first suggestion came from Mrs. Hartman; and, in consequence, she not only felt a kind of property in the scheme, but a certain right to exercise a controlling influence.

As the plan proposed to include only the orphan children of parents who had been members of the church, Mrs. Royal felt deeply interested in the subject; and as the meetings called for the consideration and adoption of measures for carrying into effect what had been proposed, were open to all the members, she attended them, and made herself clearly conversant with every plan and proposition in their minutest details.

Things had progressed as far as the appointment of lady managers, who had chosen Mrs. Hartman as President. At the minister's suggestion—he understood Mrs. Royal a great deal better than did Mrs. Hartman—the poor widow was elected to serve as a manager in the Board, much to the annoyance of the wealthy member, who really felt the appointment as a kind of degradation to herself and others; and, for a time, actually debated the question whether she should not resign, and let those who would work in that kind of humiliating association.

At the first meeting of the Board of Managers, Mrs. Hartman submitted, through a lady present, who went with her in all things, a plan for organizing the Home. According to this plan, a house was to be rented and placed in charge of a Matron, into whose care the children of the institution were to be given. A Visiting Committee were to have the supervision and direction of affairs at the Home. Then followed a detailed plan of discipline and management, in which the children were considered with about as much human regard and motherly tenderness, as if they had been mere animals, with only animal needs. This plan looked well enough on the surface, but the eyes of Mrs. Royal, made clear by love for her own precious little ones, penetrated far below the surface. In imagination, she saw them subjected to all the rigid requirements set forth in the plan of organization, and her heart sickened at the picture. She waited anxiously to hear some modifications suggested; but only words of approval were uttered.

"Perhaps," she said, at length, speaking for the first time—

Mrs. Hartman looked really surprised, and even frowned. It was presumption enough for Mrs. Royal to take her place in the Board; but to venture her opinions there, was going a little beyond decorum.

"Perhaps," suggested Mrs. Royal, "it may help us in this matter, if we think of our own children, and then seek to surround the motherless little ones, our good will designs protecting from evil and sufferings, with some of the comforts and pleasures that we could ask for them, if in like manner deprived of our love and care."

"Don't concern yourself on that head," said the lady chairman, with cold dignity, and a look of reproof. "We are Christians, and expect to do right. Damask curtains, and velvet furniture, our plan certainly does not embrace. But simple necessaries, and arrangements for health, will be provided amply."

The contrast of spirit and personal bearing between the two women, was too marked not to make its impression on the minds of the ladies present.

"These, of course, are not contemplated," calmly replied Mrs. Royal. "But, as I have intimated, it will help us in the right establishment of this Home for motherless children, if we feel *as* mothers in all we do and provide. Now, you have heard the plan of organization read, with all the details to be carried out by the Matron in charge. It sounds very well—is taking and specious. But let us go down to the particulars, and take down with us the tender little ones we have, and ask ourselves, if we could leave them in the iron boundaries of such a discipline, without a shiver in every heart-string? No, my sisters, we could not! All babes are alike precious in the eyes of God. Yours, mine, and the babes of the sad pauper who dies in the almshouse. And they are alike tender, and would be as humanely cared for, if the hearts of Christian men and women were filled with the divine love of Him who said, 'Suffer the little children to come unto me, and forbid them not, for of such is the kingdom of heaven.' Let us not, then, bind ourselves, at this early stage of proceedings, to any fixed discipline for the Home we are about to establish; but, first, select the right woman for Matron, if such a one can be found, and leave a great many little things to her loving heart, and wise perception. Pardon me, sisters, for saying so much. But, my heart is in this thing."

There was a quiver of feeling in the voice of Mrs. Royal, as she closed and sat down, that touched more than one who had listened to her earnest appeal.

"You have heard the plan of organization," said Mrs. Hartman, with something of contempt in her voice. "Shall the vote on it now be taken?"

She paused, and looked from face to face. A feeble "Aye"—"Aye"—was heard from two voices. Then all was still. Mrs. Royal's words had made no light impression. A lady, whose social position and influence in the church was in no respect inferior to that of Mrs. Hartman, now arose and said—

"Our good sister Royal has spoken well. As mothers, let us give a portion of true motherly love to the poor little ones we seek to benefit. We need not rob our own children in doing this; for God will fill our hearts even fuller of love for them. I agree with sister Royal, that much depends upon the character of the Matron we select. She should, herself, be a mother; a wise, loving, tender mother. But, where are we to find such a one?"

The lady's eyes turned, by an almost involuntary movement, towards Mrs. Royal; and others looked in the same direction. There seemed to be a common perception in the minds of a number, that she was just the woman for the place.

"Sister Royal has just said," continued the lady, "that her heart is in this thing. Why may not her hands be engaged in it, also?"

She paused again. Mrs. Hartman's face flushed, and she moved in her chair, uneasily. Her whole manner repelled the idea. The way in which Mrs. Royal received the suggestion, showed that a thought of such a thing had never crossed her mind. She was startled and embarrassed.

"What say you?" the lady addressed Mrs. Royal.

"I can say nothing," was the poor woman's answer; "because, in the first place, I have not given the subject a thought; and, in the second place, circumstances do not warrant its consideration now. Neither you nor I would be in freedom. But, as my name has, most unexpectedly, been used in this connection, and as no further proceedings can go on unembarrassed, while I remain, with permission of the President, I will retire."

Mrs. Hartman gave a stately assenting inclination of her head, and Mrs. Royal promptly withdrew.

"She is not the woman for that place," said Mrs. Hartman, in a very decided manner.

"She shall never fill it with my consent," chimed in the lady, who had offered the plan of organization.

"Nor with mine, either," said the one who had suggested the name of Mrs. Royal, "if there is anything in her character or disposition that would unfit her for so important a position. We must have the right person, and, in order to secure this, must act without fear or favor."

"My own view of the case," remarked another of the Managers, "as far as I can see, Mrs. Royal is just the woman we are in search of; though I should not have thought of proposing her; nor am

I at all certain that she will undertake so important a duty. My own impression is, that her health is too feeble."

"It is just what she wants to give her renewed health," said another. "She is killing herself with confinement over the needle. Take her out of her present life, and give her one of more scope, and increased activity of mind and body, and, my word for it, you will add ten years to her life. Leave her where she is, and in less than half of that period, you will be called on to receive her orphans into your Home."

"Then have we not a double duty before us?" queried the member who had brought the name of Mrs. Royal before the meeting. "And, indeed, is not Providence leading us into the right way. He will so lead us, if we, in heart, desire to accomplish the good thing now in our minds. Suppose, with Mrs. Royal in view, we appoint a committee of conference with our minister. He knows her better, perhaps, than any one of us."

"Not better than I do," interrupted Mrs. Hartman.

"First, then," answered the lady to this, "let us hear our President. She is not in favor of Mrs.

Royal. Of course, she must know something, that, in her mind, constitutes disqualification. She may give information that will enable us to decide at once. If Mrs. Royal is unfitted for the place of Matron, I am the last one to advocate her appointment."

Thus appealed to, Mrs. Hartman could not hold back. Yet, what had she to say? What had she to allege against Mrs. Royal?" She searched along memory's quickly-turned pages, but no pertinent facts were disclosed.

"She'll give you trouble, take my word for it, if you make this appointment," said Mrs. Hartman, with ill-concealed unkindness of feeling.

"I have known Mrs. Royal for a good many years," was the answer of a lady to this, "and I have seen nothing in her, during all that time, which has left an unfavorable impression. She is a humble-minded Christian."

"Humble minded!" echoed Mrs. Hartman. "She is anything but that. Once she did sewing for my family; but, her free, presuming way of putting herself on an equality with me, was more than I could stand. So I changed my seamstress. Humble-minded, indeed! She gave evidence of that to-day, I think."

"We are getting rather ahead of our work," suggested a member. "The question really before us is, a consideration of the plan for organizing the Home. With permission, I would move the appointment of a committee of three to consider that plan, and to confer, at the same time, with our minister."

This motion was seconded, and carried without debate.

"I now move," said the lady, "that the subject of a Matron be referred to the same committee."

This was also seconded, and carried.

"How shall that committee be appointed?" inquired Mrs. Hartman.

"I nominate Mrs. Wilkins," said a lady. Mrs. Wilkins was the member who had suggested Mrs. Royal as the right person for Matron.

"I nominate Mrs. Hartman," said another.

"Mrs. Armour," said a third.

No further nominations being made, a vote was taken, and the ladies mentioned, elected to serve on this important committee.

The first impulse of Mrs. Hartman was to decline the appointment. But a feeling of opposition to

Mrs. Royal, and a wish to prevent her election to the office of Matron evercame this impulse.

"She will never be the Matron of that Home." she said, resolutely, to herself, as she walked away from the meeting, "I'll compass heaven and earth to circumvent the scheme. Mrs. Royal!"

There was a feeling of bitter contempt in the heart of the lady.

"To set herself up to oppose and criticise *my* plan of organizing the Home; and to intimate that there was in it no Christian or motherly spirit! Humph! She expects her young hopefuls to be sent there before long, and wants damask curtains and velvet furniture. She's got above herself."

In this spirit, Mrs. Hartman returned from the meeting called to organize one of the purest charities in which the heart can engage. On her way home, it occurred to her that, as she had great influence with the minister, the first and best move for her was to see him before any other member of the Board of Managers, and get him committed to her views. So she turned aside and called upon the clergyman.

"Well," said she familiarly, and with some earnestness of manner, as soon as she was seated with him, "we have had our meeting."

"For organizing the Children's Home?"

"Yes."

"You are moving in the right direction. God's tenderest love is towards little children; and if we care for them in the right spirit, God will care for us. If even the giving of so small a thing as a cup of cold water does not lose its reward, how much of blessings may we not call down upon our souls by enlarging our charites."

Mrs. Hartman did not respond with warmth to these sentiments. She felt a little embarrassed, for the minister's words had sent a gleam of light into certain corners of her mind where dusty cobwebs hung.

"There has been a committee of conference appointed," she remarked.

"Ah! Conference with whom?"

"With yourself."

"Indeed. On what subject?"

"We wish to submit our plan of organization; and also to consult you about a Matron, in whose care the children may be placed."

"Important questions to consider," said the minister. Has any one been suggested as worthy to occupy the post of Matron?"

"Some one named Mrs. Royal," replied the lady. There were rejection and contempt in her manner.

"The very person I have had in my mind's eye from the beginning," said the minister. "If sister Royal will accept the place there is no need to seek further."

"Oh, there's no fear as to that," answered Mrs. Hartman, with ill-suppressed chagrin. "She'll jump at it."

"Then you may consider yourselves, or rather the motherless children who are to have care, protection, and love, as most fortunate. Sister Royal is a true Christian woman."

Mrs. Hartman's feelings were thrown into a state of fresh disturbance. "Is it possible," she said within herself, "that I am to be over-ridden and circumvented in this matter!"

"Perhaps," she suggested, "I may have enjoyed better opportunities for close observation than you possess."

"Not at all improbable," returned the minister. "And as it is plain that you do not favor the selection of Mrs. Royal, I hope you will speak out freely, and state your objections in all candor. In this matter, we are not to consult private feelings or prejudices, but to look to the good of those little ones intrusted to our care by God."

"In the first place," said Mrs. Hartman, in reply, "she is above herself. She doesn't know how to keep her place now; and therefore, it is plain, that if elevated to so important a trust, she will be forever intruding her own opinions, and insisting on her own views of things, and so give us endless trouble. Why, this very afternoon, the moment a carefully-digested plan of organizing the Home was offered for acceptance, she, and she only, made opposition."

"On what ground?" asked the minister.

"Oh, I can hardly remember now. Some absurd objection, I believe, about the way in which the children were to be cared for. She wanted damask curtains, velvet furniture, and all that, for them, if I understood the drift of her remarks. It was a mistake ever to have put her upon the Board of Management; and we shall have trouble so long as she is there. I, for one, don't intend bemeaning myself in any controversies with her; and if she holds her place in the Board, and is as forward as she was to day at all of our meetings, I shall resign."

The minister's aspect became grave. He looked down deeper into the lady's heart than she imagined, and saw that pride was at work far more actively than a spirit of unselfish benevolence."

"She shall never be the Matron, with my consent." Mrs. Hartman drew up her head in proud self-consciousness.

"Nor with mine," answered the minister, "unless eminently qualified for the office."

"That she is not," was the lady's positive asseveration.

"I am afraid, sister Hartman," said the minister, after musing for a little while, "that you have permitted some prejudice to creep into your mind."

"Oh, no!" Mrs. Hartman flushed a little, bridled a little, and looked a little dignified.

"Our hearts are very deceitful, sister," there was a kind smile on the minister's face, and a tone of interest in his voice—"'Deceitful,' the Bible tells us, 'and desperately wicked.' We must watch, therefore, lest its natural inclinations lead us astray.

I have already seen, that you were annoyed at the election of Mrs. Royal to a place in the management of this proposed Home; and I think, if I may speak plainly to you on the subject, as is my duty, that I have penetrated the reason thereof. But before going a step further, let me ask, my sister, whether you can bear the truth, if in that truth should come to you an accusation of wrong, both in feeling and conduct?"

"Oh, I am not perfect; I am only human," said Mrs. Hartman, in reply, her manner becoming much disturbed.

"God looks into our very thoughts; yea, and below these, to the secert impulses of feeling that quicken them into life," remarked the teacher, impressively. "He knows us better than we know ourselves. He is not a respecter of persons, nor a regarder of position or worldly influence. Hath he not chosen the poor of this world, rich in faith, and heirs of the kingdom? Are not all little children precious in his sight?"

The minister paused, and the eyes of his listener fell beneath his earnest look.

"Sister Hartman," resumed the minister impressively, "I fear that the earthly good things poured so bountifully into your lap by a kind Providence, have been regarded as evidences of superior goodness on your part; and that you have suffered that dangerous enemy, spiritual pride, to creep in and blind you to real good in others, who walk in humbler paths. I know Mrs. Royal well. For years I have noted her incomings and her outgoings. I have seen her in the midst of sore trials, and under the pressure of heavy burdens. Yet, was she always patient, kind, enduring and self-denying. Steadily has she moved onwards, keeping the quiet tenor of her way; faithful to all duties; even-tempered; unobtrusive, yet never losing her womanly self-respect. In a word, Mrs. Hartman, her life, as I have read it, and my opportunities have been large, has been the life of a Christian. Can more be asked?"

"I think," said Mrs. Hartman, not disposed to let her minister have it all his own way, "that for a woman in her station, Mrs. Royal is entirely too forward. She meets you, with the equal air of any lady in the land. And yet she is only a sewing-woman. I quit giving her work, on this very account. Her manner always annoyed me. Why, she would 'sister Hartman' me, with the sewing in her hand!"

"Is that so?" asked the minister, in a tone of surprise.

"Indeed it is so!" replied Mrs. Hartman, entirely mistaking the tenor of her minister's thoughts. "And it was very annoying. She did it once, before a lady visitor, and I was mortified to death about it. I made up my mind, then, that she and I would have to walk by different ways through the world; and it has been so ever since."

"There is only one safe way through the world, Mrs. Hartman," said the minister, "and by that way all must go who expect to gain heaven at the journey's end. Sister Royal, I think, is in the right way—the way of duty, self-denial, and humility. You, I fear, have wandered a little."

"Me!" Mrs. Hartman felt this to be almost an outrage. Mrs. Royal on the road to heaven, and she astray! Now, that was going too far.

"All souls, remember," said the minister, with impressive force, "are equal in the sight of God, who never regards the worldly position of any one. The wife of Edward Hartman is no more in His eyes, than the humble widow who makes her garments; nay, nor of so much value, if the humble widow be richer than she in the possession of heavenly graces. To think thus, may hurt the low false pride of our evil hearts; but, if we assume to be Christian men and women, let us conform our lives to the pure doctrines of the Gospel. If we do not, our religion is vain, and we are deceiving ourselves."

Before Mrs. Hartman retired from the minister's she understood the true quality of her affections a great deal better than when she called in order to commit him, if possible, to her side of the Matron question. He had faithfully done his duty by her, influential as she was in the church, and dangerous as an opponent; and there was just good enough left in her to react under the probe of his sharply cutting words. He called upon her, early the next morning, in some concern of mind for the result of his plain speaking. Mrs. Hartman was sober and reserved, but not repellent; and there was about her something of the air of one who had suffered humiliation of spirit.

At the next meeting of the Board of Managers, the minister was present by invitation. Mrs. Royal did not attend. When the name of the poor sewing-woman was introduced in connection with the office of Matron for the Orphans' Home, only a feeble opposition was made on the part of one lady. In contrast to this, was testimony in her favor of the strongest character—so strong, that Mrs. Hartman felt rebuked by its accumulation in the face of her previous opposition. When the vote was taken on a motion to fill the office of Matron, not a single "nay" was heard.

The result proved the wisdom of this choice. The Home was at once organized, and Mrs. Royal placed in charge of the motherless little ones who were gathered within its sheltering walls. But, it took Mrs. Hartman a long time to get wholly reconciled. She still held her place as President of the Board, and was on the Visiting Committee; and tried to feel kindly towards Mrs. Royal, as was her duty as a Christian woman. But she was annoyed when the Matron assumed to differ with her in anything pertaining to the children—the more so, as it almost always happened that the other ladies of the committee saw things with the Matron's eyes rather than with hers. There was a social gulf between them, which Mrs. Hartman would not have passed, and every seeming attempt on the part of Mrs. Royal to bridge it over, was felt as a presumption that must be repelled.

But, self-discipline was going on. Mrs. Hartman had some earnestness of purpose, and some yearnings after a Christian life. The discipline of time and circumstances was doing its work, and the Divine Providence, which is intimate with every one from the cradle to the grave, so reacting upon her, at every step of her way, that, through pain of mind and pain of body, she was becoming purified and meet for the kingdom.

Ah! how full of Mrs. Hartmans are all of our churches; and how severe must be the humiliating discipline that is to make them lowly in mind as true disciples! It is hard, very hard, for human pride to bend its neck for the Gospel yoke. Hard for the lofty to sit down, side by side with the humble follower of the meek and lowly Saviour. And yet, to be greatest of all is to be servant of all. Alas! with what darkness of interior vision do we read the doctrines of Life!

XXIII.

AUNTY JONES, THE PEACEMAKER.

Aunty Jones—she was called "Aunty" by half the village, old and young, though she claimed with no individual in Bloomingdale a blood relationship.—Aunty Jones was sitting by the window of her neat little cottage home, when a neighbor entered through the white-washed gate, and came with a quick step along the flower-bordered walk that led up to the door.

"Good afternoon, Aunty," said she, entering without ceremony.

"Good afternoon, Mrs. Blake! How are all at home?"

"Well, thank you. How are you to-day?"

"As well as usual, dear; take a chair."

Mrs. Blake sat down. She was a young woman with rather a smart air, and free manners. Her eyes were black, and had a good deal of latent fire in them. After a few remarks, she said, with considerable animation:

"There's trouble between Mrs. Fry and Mrs. Lingen."

"Indeed! I'm sorry for that," said Aunty Jones, a shade of regret passing over her countenance. "What's the matter?"

"Mrs. Fry is greatly to blame," said Mrs. Blake, "and I don't wonder that Mrs. Lingen is angry. I should be if I were in her place."

"What has happened to interrupt the good understanding that has always existed between them? They've been fast friends for years."

"I know they have," answered Mrs. Blake. "But after what Mrs. Fry has done, it is impossible for them to be friends any longer."

"What has she done?" Aunty Blake looked seriously troubled.

"I'll tell you," said Mrs. Blake, speaking in her animated way, and entering with much feeling into the relation: "Willy Lingen was over at Mrs. Fry's this morning, playing with her children. The little folks had a falling out about something, as children will fall out, you know, and from angry words came to blows. Hearing the noise and outcry that followed, Mrs. Fry ran out the garden, and, in a fit of passion, seized Willy Lingen by the hair, and boxed his ears like a fury. He, poor child, as it happened, had been sick all last night with the ear-ache, and the side of his face and head were tender as a boil, and badly swollen. He was, in consequence, hurt terribly. Of course, he came home and told his mother, and, of course, she was outraged, as any mother would be. She didn't stop a moment for reflection, but went, in hot haste, over to Mrs. Fry's, and gave her a piece of her mind in about the plainest kind of terms."

"Bad—bad—very bad," said Aunty Jones, shaking her head.

"I've just come from Mrs. Lingen's," continued Mrs. Blake; "and, I can tell you, she's as sharp as an awl about it—and a little sharper. Poor Willy shows signs of his hard treatment. Dear little fellow! It made my blood boil when his mother told me of the cruel way in which he had been served. Some of the neighbors blame her for what she said to Mrs. Fry, but I don't. I would have said as much, and, maybe, twice as much more, if I had been in her place. Beat a neighbor's child about the head, and pull its hair, when her own brats, in all probability, were most to blame! According to Willy's story, he was only defending himself when she came at him like a tiger."

After Mrs. Blake had fully informed Aunty Jones as to this new cause of excitement in the village, she bade her a good afternoon, and went on her gossiping round of visits. Not long after her departure, Aunty Jones had another call. It was from a neighbor in the opposite interest—a friend to Mrs. Fry, whose house she had left a little while before. Her version of the affair differed considerably from that given by Mrs. Blake, with the exception of the part about Mrs. Lingen's indignation visit to the house of Mrs. Fry—which was given with some added incidents and a higher coloring.

"Mrs. Fry did just as I would have done, had I been in her place," said she, warmly. "The children were playing together, when Mrs. Fry heard her little Katy scream out suddenly; running into the garden, she saw Willy Lingen with her finger in his mouth. He got angry with her about something, and snapped at her finger like a dog! Mrs. Fry caught hold of him, and ordered him to let go instantly. But the young savage held on, and she did just as I or you would have done, boxed his ears until he was glad to let go; when he ran off home, bellowing like a calf, and told his mother some lie about it."

"Bad—bad—very bad!" Aunty Jones shook her head as before, and looked quite sorrowful about the matter.

"Of course," said the neighbor, "they will be bitter enemies till they die. Quarrels about children are generally of the worst kind."

"I hope not," said Aunty Jones. "We must forgive, if we would be forgiven."

"They'll never forgive each other. How can they?" remarked the neighbor. "If you'd heard the way in which Mrs. Lingen talked to Mrs. Fry, you'd see that it was impossible. Mrs. Lingen is not the woman to make apologies; and it would take a book-full to satisfy the lady she was pleased to outrage by all sorts of disgraceful epithets; even going so far as to throw up things that happened long before Mrs. Fry was married."

"I'm very sorry." Aunty Jones had no words to utter but words of regret.

"Do you blame Mrs. Fry for being outraged?" The neighbor tried to get Aunty Jones committed to her side of the question.

"In all quarrels among neighbors, there is usually faults on both sides." This was as far as she would go.

"I can't see what fault there was on the side of Mrs. Fry," was answered with considerable warmth. "Suppose it had been your child instead of Mrs. Fry's, wouldn't you have boxed the ears of the young savage who was biting her finger, to compel him to let go? My word for it, you would, Aunty Jones; you are not a stock or a stone."

But Aunty Jones admitted no imaginary action of her own, by way of justification in the case of Mrs. Fry. She had only regrets to utter. Before night, several neighbors called in to talk the matter over with Aunty Jones, each one having a slightly different version of the affair, and each being warmly committed to one side or the other. Mrs. Frick always knew that Willy Lingen was one of the worst children in Bloomingdale, and as for his mother, it was only necessary to look into her face to see that she was a Tartar. For her part, she fully justified Mrs. Fry, and had told her so. Mrs. Camp had seen Mrs. Lingen, and examined poor, dear Willy's head. None but a savage, in her opinion, could have so cruelly maltreated a child. It was well known that Mrs. Fry was a woman of most ungovernable temper, and beat her own children awfully. Indeed, she had heard it whispered—and she repeated the rumor in a confidential whisper—that she had even struck her husband in a fit of passion.

Aunty Jones was grieved to the heart. To all of this she answered but little, except to suggest that there must be exaggeration on both sides, and that if the exact truth could be brought to the light, it would, in all probability, be found, that both of the exasperated mothers had been excited into a blind passion by falsehood, over-acting, or misrepresentation on the part of the children. The two neighbors, so suddenly set at variance, were, both of them, her warm friends, and had been on terms of close intimacy with each other for years. Both were, in the main, kind-hearted and right-minded women; and both of them, Aunty Jones believed, would soon be sorry for what they had done, and ashamed of having taken counsel of passion. She was the peacemaker of Bloomingdale; and even in this bad-looking case, was soon pondering the question of reconciliation.

On the next morning, Aunty Jones went over

early to see Mrs. Lingen. She had thought it best to give her the benefit of a night's sleep on the matter. She found her strongly exasperated against Mrs. Fry. Willy's inflamed ear was shown in triumphant vindication of her right to be angry. Aunty Jones examined the ear, but could not find any very decided marks of inflammation. There was, just within the opening, a little deeper tinge, and on the back of the ear, close to the head, a spot of darker hue, that, if she saw right, came from a little cluster of pimples. Willy had all the appearance of a suffering martyr, as Mrs. Lingen exhibited him in evidence of the wrong done to her mother's heart, and in justification of her indignant assault upon Mrs. Fry.

"Willy," said Aunty Jones, as he stood before her, with one of his little hands held in one of hers, and her kind, yet earnest eyes, looking right into his—"Willy, what was Katy Fry doing to you, when you got her finger into your mouth?"

Mrs. Lingen gave a start at this question, and Willy's face crimsoned. A glance from Aunty Jones kept the mother silent.

"You didn't bite Katy's finger hard, I hope, Willy?"

"No ma'am!" Willy's face was redder still, as he made this admission.

"What made you bite her finger, Willy?"—Aunty Jones spoke so very kindly, and yet so earnestly, keeping the child's eyes fixed in hers all the time that no chance was left for anything but truthful answers.

"Because she was trying to take my apple from me, and wouldn't let go. But I didn't bite it hard, Aunty Jones; and Mrs. Fry had no business to box me on my sore ear as she did." Willy closed this defence by bursting into tears.

Enough, however, had been elicited to place the whole matter in an entirely new light before his mother's eyes. She told the weeping child to leave the room, and, as soon as he had done so, said to her visitor:

"This is all new to me, Aunty Jones. It is the first intimation I have had of any finger-biting in the case."

"I am told," replied Aunty Jones, "that Willy bit Katy's finger very badly; and that Mrs. Fry had to box his ears several times, very severely before he would let go. If this is the case—and Willy admits that he did bite the finger—can you greatly wonder at Mrs. Fry? Reverse the case. Think how you would act, if you were to find a neighbor's child biting Willy's finger, and your child screaming in pain. Would you stay your hand an instant?"

The countenance of Mrs. Lingen fell. All indignation died out of her heart. She stood rebuked in the presence of Aunty Jones, like one convicted of a great wrong.

"Would you, Mrs. Lingen?" Aunty Jones pressed her last query.

"No, not for an instant!" was the firm reply.

A broad smile lit up the fine face of Aunty Jones, as she reached out her hand, and said:

"There spoke out the true woman! I knew your heart was in the right place. And I have not lost faith in Mrs. Fry. Neither of you is capable of wantonly hurting a child—neither of wantonly outraging the other. There does not exist the slightest reason why you should not be friends as of old."

"Oh yes, there does," was firmly answered.

"What reason?"

"I don't believe she will ever forgive me for what I said to her, yesterday, in the heat of passion."

"Yes, she will. Leave that to me. When she understands how the matter was presented to your mind, she will not wonder that you were provoked; and the slightest apology on your part, will make all right again."

"I can't believe it," said Mrs. Lingen.

"I am sure of it," replied Aunty Jones, confidently.

And, in less than an hour she had the two old friends face to face again, bathed in tears of reconciliation.

Blessings on Aunty Jones! She was the peacemaker of Bloomingdale. Neighbors would fall out, and busy-bodies would make wider every breach; but Aunty Jones was always true to her mission—always on hand to throw oil upon the troubled waves of passion. She knew that there was honor, and truth, and right purposes in every heart, as well as selfishness and blind passion; and her hands never rested when she saw the latter obscuring the former, until the dimming veil was rent asunder.

Would that every village and neighborhood had its Aunty Jones.

XXIV.

WHICH SHALL SERVE?

THERE is natural life, into which we are born naturally; and there is spiritual life, which has its beginning in the new birth of divine affections; and the problem of religion is, Which shall serve? Both cannot rule in the mind: one must be servant to the other. The natural mind must give up its evil inclinations, in obedience to the higher laws of spiritual life; or the spiritual must yield to the natural, and become its slave; and then the man's last state is worse than the first.

So the teacher taught; and with the sentiment clearly discriminated in his mind, Mr. Loring took his way homeward from church, pondering the lesson he had heard. It did not pass from his thoughts, like a vision of the night. He turned it over and over, and viewed it from all sides; and the longer he dwelt upon it, the more palpable it became.

"So here is the sum and substance of religion, expressed in a formula," he said, as he talked with himself. "The question is, Which shall rule, and which obey? All is resolved into the simplest elements. What remains beyond is to discriminate between the natural and the spiritual; and on this point the preacher's instruction was clear. 'The natural man,' said he, 'is selfish, proud, cruel, and revengeful; but the spiritual man is a lover of his neighbor, whose good he seeks; is humble, forgiving, just, and self-denying. There is not much danger of a mistake here. There is little room left for any confounding of ideas. The antithesis is complete."

Mr. Loring was a man just beginning to be in earnest on the subject of religion. He went to church, and read his Bible and religious books, because he wished to know the laws of spiritual life. He read a great deal that was mere generalization, and listened to a great deal of abstract discussion of theological questions; but these did not help him. He wanted the thing narrowed down to a simple formula, suited to all conditions of life, and ready for use at any and all times; and he had it now, in the proposition—Which shall serve?

On Monday morning, Mr. Loring went to his store, and began the business duties of another week. He was a man of clear thought, active will, and enduring purpose. Whatever he put his hand to had to move. He generally saw right to the completion of a thing, and worked towards that completion by the quickest means and the readiest way. It was this element in his character that would not let him be satisfied with any vague, dark things in religion. He wanted no "mysteries," but a light set on a bushel, or a city on a hill.

Among the business letters received on that day was one from a southern customer, ordering several bales of a certain kind of goods, if to be had at quotations of a specified date, the latest at which he had received the prices current at New York. Now, the market was unchanged; but Mr. Loring knew certain holders of the goods who had recently suffered a heavy loss, and were not, therefore, in any condition to carry stock.

"I'll make something handsome out of this order," said Mr. Loring to himself, in an animated way. "It comes in the nick of time. Austin & Ledon are in a corner, and to make a sale of this extent, will come down through quite a range of figures."

So, after transacting some preliminary business, Mr. Loring, quite elated in mind at the prospect of so profitable an operation, left his place of business, and went to the store of Austin & Ledon. In rather an indifferent way—the manner assumed, of course—he asked the price of the article he had come prepared to buy.

"How much do you want?" inquired Mr. Ledon, the younger partner of the firm.

"That will depend something upon the price," answered Mr. Loring, with evasion.

"There has been no change in quotations for some weeks, and the stock in first hands is not large."

"Are there not several heavy shipments on the way?" Queried Mr. Loring.

A shadow glided across the face of Mr. Ledon. Mr. Loring saw it, and with a feeling of satisfaction.

"I have not heard of them," replied Mr. Ledon.

"I think, on inquiry, that you will find my intimations correct. I was at Baker & Brothers yesterday, and noticed a pile of invoices on their desk.

The steamer's letters had just arrived; and you know that they are extensive operators in the article."

"Yes; I know." There was a shade of despondency in the tones of Mr. Ledon.

"I will take twenty bales, if I can get them right," said the bargaining purchaser.

"You shall have them right," was the emphatic answer. "Let me say a word to Mr. Austin."

After a brief consultation with his partner, Mr. Ledon returned to Mr. Loring, and named a price which was at least five per cent. below the regular quotations.

But Mr. Loring looked grave, and shook his head. And now, the senior partner, anxious to make so important a sale, came out from the counting-room."

"Not temptation enough," said Mr. Loring, addressing himself to Mr. Austin.

"The price we have quoted is only a fraction above cost," replied the merchant. "Indeed, when interest and storage are added, the margin left to us will be scarcely discernible."

Now, Mr. Loring had fixed in his mind a reduction of ten per cent. below quotations. This would give him a clear gain of a hundred and fifty dol lars besides commissions. Already, in fancy, he had added that sum to the day's earnings; and to abate a single dime thereof seemed like an actual loss.

"I think I had better hold on a few days," said he, indifferently. "The present rates cannot be sustained. I have no doubt, but that Barker & Brothers have large invoices on the way. It will be safer for me to see them first, at any rate."

The partners glanced at each other, uneasily, then drew aside and talked together in a low tone. Mr. Loring heard the words—

"We cannot afford to lose this sale"—"Needs are too pressing"—"Shall sustain a loss, if we recede farther"—"Mustn't let him go to Barker's."

"The fact is, Mr. Loring," said Mr. Austin, the senior partner, speaking in a sober, yet frank way—"Our recent heavy loss has rather tied up our hands, and cut off our resources. But for this, we would not have named anything below market rates. You want twenty bales?"

"Yes, I would take twenty, if the price suited."

Mr. Austin stood in thought for a few minutes, and then gave a price that exactly suited the views of Mr. Loring, who ordered the goods sent to his store.

"That will do for one transaction," said the shrewd merchant, as he walked back to his place of business. "I can afford to sit with idle hands for the rest of the day."

After the pleasurable excitement occasioned by this piece of bargain-making had subsided, Mr. Loring was conscious of an uncomfortable pressure on his feelings. He was not altogether at ease in his mind. Something had jarred the machinery ot his life. What could it be?—from whence was the element of disturbance? What was its nature? Mr. Loring turned back his thoughts upon the morning's incidents; but failed to discover the cause.

In the course of the day, the goods bought from Austin & Ledon were sent in, and the invoice laid on the desk of Mr. Loring. As his eyes rested on the footing up, and he made a hurried calculation of his profit in the transaction, he felt a renewed glow of pleasure; but this soon went down again, and the uncomfortable feeling returned. The pressure still remained at the close of business hours, and he took it home with him.

"What is the meaning of this?" he said within himself, as he sat alone, after tea, in anything but a pleasant frame of mind. "I have no cause to complain of the day's business. My profit has largely exceeded that of any other this season."

Then, as he sat musing, his thoughts returned to the subject which had so much interested him on the day before, and the query, "Which shall serve?" again arrested his attention.

"Ah! That is the touch-stone," he said. "Let me examine my day's work, and see how it will bear the test."

Of course, the leading transaction came up first.

"Which served here, the spiritual or the natural?" He asked the question with some firmness.

But, there was, for a little while, a bewilderment. He could not see clearly. All the elements of his mind were thrown into temporary confusion.

"There is a divine standard," he said, resolutely to himself, at last, "and the quality of all actions must be determined by this. 'As ye would that men should do unto you, do ye even so to them.' Did I observe this Golden Rule in that transaction? Let me reverse the positions of all parties. Ah, no! I see it clearly now. I would not have thought it right in Austin & Ledon to take from me the fair profit on my goods, because a necessity, which I could not shun, placed me in their hands. And now, the question comes up again, "Which served here, the spiritual or the natural?"

Mr. Loring bowed his head and sat musing on the proposition. "The natural man," so his thought run, "is selfish, proud, and cruel; the spiritual man a lover of the neighbor, just and self-denying."

The difference was very clearly marked. There could be no danger of error.

"Which served?" Mr. Loring was in so earnest a frame of mind, that he spoke aloud. There was a pause. Specious reasonings began to intrude themselves, and self-interest to lift a blinding veil. In the strife that now began, Mr. Loring started to his feet, and commenced pacing the floor.

"You cannot bring this law down into ordinary business transactions. It would be suicidal," said self-interest. "There must be a great change in the world, before a man is able to live up to the Gospel standard in trade."

But enlightened reason saw the fallacy of this, as applied to the case on hand, and answered it by the question—

"Did I act upon the 'let live,' as well as the 'live' principle, in the present case? No; I did not!" was the emphatic response; "but instead, coveted my neighbor's goods, and used deceiving arts, in order to obtain them! I was not content to make a fair profit, in an honorable transaction; but, discovering my neighbor's necessities, took advantage of them, to secure for myself what of right was his. Which served in this case?"

Mr. Loring paused, and stood still; then resolutely answered to himself.

"The spiritual served! The higher principle stooped down and degraded itself, as a servant to the lower. Neighborly love became passive, that self-love might rule. Good gave place to evil!"

"This will not do," he resumed, after standing silent for some moments. "If I wish to turn my steps heavenward, I must seek another way; for all progress in this direction must be downwards instead of upwards. The order of life must be reversed. Natural, selfish affections must be servant to spiritual and divine affections. Religion is life, and life is action; a religious life must, therefore, be a good life."

But natural affections were not thus to be overcome by a single effort. The life of self-love is strong in the heart of every man; for it has been stimulated, from childhood up, with an abundance of the most nutritious food. The forces of evil rallied again; and, for a time, Mr. Loring's clear perceptions were dimmed, and he felt weak in the hands of the enemies of his soul. Then, in conscious weakness and fear, he looked upwards and prayed for wisdom and strength—for clear sight and unflinching purpose.

"I have done evil," he said now to himself, "and have sinned against God; but I repent."

"Then do the works meet for repentance." The injunction was in his own thought, and he answered —"I will!"

When Mr. Loring became really in earnest in a matter, he was no half-way man. From this point he refused to listen to the pleadings and demands of natural principles, and steadily maintained a better resolution. On the next day he drew up the notes to be given for the goods purchased of Austin & Ledon, and made them for an amount equal to the price of the goods at current quotations.

"You have made an error," said Mr. Austin, as he looked at the face of the notes.

"I am aware of that," replied Mr. Loring, "and simply correct it now. I have ascertained that Barker & Brother have no shipments on the way, as I intimated yesterday. The goods will not, I presume, recede, but rather advance in the next sixty days. So I consider it only fair to let you make your profit, and I will be content with mine."

"You are a strange man," said Mr. Austin, taken altogether by surprise.

"How so?" was the quiet interrogation.

"It is now thirty years since I began business in this city," replied Austin, "and this is the first instance within my knowledge of a merchant's receding, to his own disadvantage, from a good bargain."

"Am I wrong?" inquired Mr. Loring.

"You are just," said the other.

"Then I am right; for if this be just, the opposite would be unjust."

"I am not sure, however," said Mr. Austin, "that we can accept your generous concession. We sold the goods at a price agreed upon, and we preferred selling to keeping them in store. It was a fair business transaction."

"You cannot hold me to an unjust thing," replied Mr. Loring. "According to your own view of the case, my offer to pay the regular market price you considered an act of justice. To settle, according to the original agreement, would, therefore, involve injustice on my part, and leave my conscience troubled."

"Have it your own way; have it your own way, Mr. Loring!" Austin replied, with some feeling. "This is, indeed, a new thing under the sun. The millennium is at hand!"

Mr. Loring smiled, and said—

"Is it so strange a thing, then, for men to be simply just in business?"

"It is, in my experience," replied Mr. Austin. "Every man goes in for himself; and in going in for himself, ignores the interest of his neighbor. Get what you can, through any modes of sharp bargaining not hindered by law, and keep all you get. This is the mercantile creed of to-day. And I do not afirm that I have acted, in all of my dealings, very far away from this creed. But, Mr. Loring, your conduct a little staggers my faith in myself. It is just, I see; but I am not sure that I could have done so nobly. I honor you as a Christian merchant, and wish from my heart that the world were full of such."

And he caught the hand of Mr. Loring in his enthusiasm, and clasped it with a firm pressure.

"We call ourselves Christian men," said Mr. Loring; "but can we be Christian men if we are not Christian merchants? Is any man entitled to the name who narrows down his purposes to the little item of self, as if he were of most importance in the world? I think not. There must be just action towards others, or there can be no Christianity in the heart."

"The doctrine is clear," replied Mr. Austin; "and I thank you for both the true precept and the good action. I think the profit will be mine as well as yours."

After that Mr. Loring walked in a broader light, and with a firmer step. The way before him was plainer. He saw, clearly discriminated, the difference between natural and spiritual principles; and elected, that in his mind the spiritual should not serve, but rule; and it was so.

XXV.

MR. BROWNLEE'S VISITOR.

Mr. Brownlee felt comfortable. It was evening, and late in December. Outside, the wind had a cold, sharp whistle, and the snow, with which it was laden, had been weaving, since early morning, a shroud for the waning year. Within, the grate glowed, the gas burned brilliantly, wife smiled, and children played in happy unconsciousness of cold, or want, or suffering.

Mr. Brownlee was in his pleasant sitting-room, the walls of which were hung with pictures, the windows draped with curtains, and the floor carpeted with yielding Brussels. He sat by a centre table, on which were new books and the latest numbers of the best monthlies.

Now, all this was calculated to make a man feel comfortable; and Mr. Brownlee was entitled to what he enjoyed; for he was an honorable, intelligent, active, and successful merchant, a good citizen, a loving husband, and a wise and tender parent.

"Wasn't that our bell?" Mr. Brownlee asked, looking up from the page of a book.

"I think so," answered Mrs. Brownlee, and both listened as the waiter moved along the passage. A man's voice was heard.

"I shouldn't wonder," said Mr. Brownlee, "if that were Mr. Lewis." There was a shade of dissatisfaction in his tones.

"Mr. Lewis," said the waiter, entering the sitting-room a few moments afterwards.

"Ask him to walk up stairs."

The waiter retired. Mr. and Mrs. Brownlee looked at each other; but as their children were present, neither made any remark. But it was understood between them that the visit of Mr. Lewis was mutually regarded as something bordering on an intrusion. They were feeling very comfortable, as we have seen, shut in from the chilling wintry blasts, and with the most agreeable surroundings; and the presence of any stranger, just at that time, could scarcely help being unwelcome.

"Good evening, Mr. Lewis." Mr. Brownlee's voice was kind, if not cordial.

A man plainly, we might say coarsely, dressed entered the room. His manners were far from being polished; though his rather pale, care-worn face had in it many indications of a natural refinement.

"Good evening," he responded, giving an awkward nod. "Good evening, ma'am," was added, with a nod, in turn, to Mrs. Brownlee. And then he came forwards and took the chair that was offered him, and drawing up to the grate, warmed himself.

"Heavy storm this," remarked Mr. Brownlee.

"Yes. The snow lies over a foot deep. But you are very comfortable here." And Mr. Lewis glanced around the pleasant room.

"How is your wife to day?" inquired Mrs. Brownlee.

"Something better, thank you, ma'am. I hav'n't been able to see her; but the nurse told me that she slept last night, and has less fever to-day. I feel very much encouraged. Oh, dear! If she only gets over it, I shall be so rejoiced!"

"How many children have you?"

"Four, ma'am; and the youngest is just about as old as that dear little girl now in your lap. Oh, dear! It was hard for her to be separated from her mother, but harder for the mother. I'm so in hopes she'll get safely over it soon. I talked with the doctor to-day; and he says that he's no doubt all will come out right."

"I hope so, indeed," said Mrs. Brownlee, kindly.

"How pleasant it is here!" and Mr. Lewis looked all around the room again. "And you are so happy in having all your children around you! Home is a blessed place—blessed, even though homely. Mine wasn't like this; but it was a happy home for all that."

"Where are your children now?"

"Scattered all around among relations—poor things! Since my wife's sickness, it's taken all I had saved, and all I could earn, to get her doctored. Oh, if they should cure her now, I shall be so happy!"

"We will hope for the best," said Mr. Brownlee.

"I always do that; but it has been hoping against hope for the last eight or nine months. The darkest hour, they tell us, is just before day-break. So I comfort myself with thinking the morning is very near."

Mr. and Mrs. Brownlee were touched with the earnestness and simple pathos of their visitor, a poor man from the country, who had brought his wife to one of the city hospitals to be cured, if possible, of a disease that for a time threatened her life. Mr. Brownlee had met him by accident, and from kindness of heart invited him to his house. Mr. Lewis had taken advantage of this invitation to drop in two or three times a week and enjoy the home comforts and the books and periodicals he found in Mr. Brownlee's pleasant sitting-room. He was not always an entirely welcome guest; and yet he was so simple-minded, so interested with the children, and manifested so much enjoyment in the books and magazines he found upon the centre table, that neither Mr. Brownlee nor his wife could feel anything but kindness towards their unsophisticated intruder.

On the present occasion, Mr. Lewis, after warming himself by the grate, talking for a time in his own peculiar way, and amusing himself with the children, took up a book, and was soon buried in its pages. Time went gliding by on swift wings, and Mr. Lewis took no notice of his flight. Nine o'clock came, and the last child was put to bed, but he went on turning the pages of the book in which he had become interested, wholly unconscious that the long evening had waned so far. Half-past nine found him still buried in its pages.

Mr. Brownlee, who had for a time felt pleasure in the poor man's enjoyment of his comfortable surroundings, now began wishing him away.

"I like to be hospitable," he said to himself, "but this is carrying the joke a little too far."

Ten o'clock was rung out at last by the handsome French clock on the mantel-piece, but Mr. Lewis did not heed the warning.

"This is a very interesting book," he said, about five minutes afterwards, looking at Mr. Brownlee, his mild face beaming with true enjoyment. "How pleasant it is here!" he added; and then his eyes went back to the page from which he had lifted them.

Mr. Brownlee's heart softened towards the poor man, and yet he could not overcome a feeling of annoyance at his prolonged stay. He looked at his wife, and his wife looked at him—then they glanced mutually and meaningly at Mr. Lewis. Mrs. Brownlee yawned, and Mr. Brownlee yawned, rather loudly, in concert; but their guest was wholly oblivious. The fascination of the page was complete. Next, Mr. Brownlee got up, and commenced pacing the floor; he was too fidgety to sit still. He looked at the clock, the minute-hand of which was now almost at thirty, looked at Mr. Lewis, looked at his wife, knit his brows, and then walked on more rapidly than before. At last impatience spoke out.

"Mr. Lewis," said he, "do you know how late it is?" Now, Mr. Brownlee tried to say this with some gentleness; but his real feelings came more fully into his voice than he was aware. It was plain, from the shadow that came instantly over the face of Mr. Lewis, as he closed the book, and let it fall upon the table, that he felt rebuked. His eyes glanced from the countenance of Mr. Brownlee to the clock on the mantel.

"Half-past ten!" he said, in surprise. "I didn't dream of its being so late. Time passes much quicker here, I think, than it does in some other places. Good evening, sir! Good evening, ma'am! I shall remember your kindness as long as I live. I should not have staid so late; but a book and this pleasant room made me forget myself. At the cheap tavern where I am staying, there is no place to sit down in but the bar; and I don't like drinking, smoking, and swearing. I walk the streets half of the evening, sometimes; but to-night it was too stormy. Good evening, sir. Good evening, ma'am."

And Mr. Lewis turned away, and went forth into the blinding storm, to walk nearly half a mile before gaining his dreary lodging-place.

"Poor man!" there was pity in the voice of Mrs. Brownlee.

"And yet," said Mr. Brownlee, speaking in answer to the words of Mr. Lewis, rather than to those of his wife, "I gave him grudgingly of my home-comforts, and suffered a weak, selfish annoyance, while he was drinking in pleasure at every source! What a storm it is!" Mr. Brownlee glanced towards the window, against which had come the snow-laden blast with a heavier rush. "And I have sent this poor man forth to meet its wintry chill, with a pressure on his feelings. A little more Christian patience, a little more consideration, a little more unselfish pleasure in sharing my good gifts with him, would have made his spirit lighter, and mine also. Kindness, humanity, regard for others, ever bear a double blessing; the want of them as surely lays upon our hearts a double burden. I was never more conscious of this than now. I will try not to forget the lesson. The lighting of another's candle at ours should never dim its radiance, as it has dimmed mine to-night."

XXVI.

THE SHADOWS WE CAST.

A CHILD was playing with some building blocks; and, as the mimic castle rose before his eyes in graceful proportions, a new pleasure swelled in his heart. He felt himself to be the creator of a "thing of beauty," and was conscious of a new-born power. Arch, wall, buttress, gateway, draw-bridge, lofty tower, and battlement were all the work of his hands. He was in wonder at his own skill in thus creating, from an unseemly pile of blocks, a structure of such rare design.

Silently he stood and gazed upon his castle, with something like the pride of an architect who sees, after months or years of skillfully applied labor, some grand conception in his art, embodied in imperishable stone. Then he moved around, viewing it on every side. It did not seem to him a toy, reaching only a few inches in height, and covering but a square foot of ground, but a real castle, lifting itself hundreds of feet upwards towards the blue sky, and spreading wide upon the earth its ample foundations. As the idea grew more and more perfect, his strange pleasure increased. Now he stood, with folded arms, wrapped in the overmastering illusion—now walked slowly around, viewing the structure on all sides, and noting every minute particular—and now sat down, and bent over it with the fondness of a mother bending over her child. Again he arose, purposing to obtain another and more distant view of his work. But his foot struck against one of the buttresses, and instantly, with a crash, wall, tower, and battlement fell in hopeless ruin!

In the room, with the boy sat his father, reading. The crash disturbed him; and he uttered a sharp, angry rebuke, glancing, for a moment, towards the startled child, and then returning his eyes to the attractive page before him, unconscious of the shadow he had cast upon the heart of his child. Tears came into those fair blue orbs, dancing in light a moment before. From the frowning face of his father, to which his glance was suddenly turned, the child looked back to the shapeless ruins of his castle. Is it any wonder that he bowed his face in silence upon them, and wet them with his tears.

For more than five minutes, he sat as still as if sleeping; then, in a mournful kind of way, yet almost noiselessly, he commenced restoring to the box, from which he had taken them, the many-shaped pieces that, fitly joined together, had grown into a noble building. After the box was filled, he replaced the cover, and laid it carefully upon a shelf in the closet.

Poor child! That shadow was a deep one, and long in passing away. His mother found him, half an hour afterwards, asleep on the floor, with cheeks flushed to an unusual brightness. She knew nothing of that troubled passage in his young life; and the father had forgotten, in the attractions of his book, the momentary annoyance, expressed in words and tones with a power in them to shadow the heart of his child.

A young wife had busied herself for many days in preparing a pleasant surprise for her husband. The work was finished at last; and now she awaited his return, with a heart full of warm emotions. A dressing-gown, and pair of elegantly embroidered slippers, wrought by her own skillful fingers, were the gifts with which she meant to delight him. What a troop of pleasant fancies was in her heart! How, almost impatiently, did she wait for the coming twilight, which was to be dawn, not approaching darkness, to her!

A last, she heard the step of her husband in the passage, and her pulses leaped with fluttering delight. Like a bird upon the wing, she almost flew down to meet him, impatient for the kiss that awaited her.

To men in the world of business, few days pass without their disappointments and perplexities. It is man's business to bear this in a manly spirit. They form but a portion of life's discipline, and should make them stronger, braver, and more enduring. Unwisely, and we may say unjustly, too many men fail to leave their business cares and troubles in their stores, workshops, or counting-rooms, at the day's decline. They wrap them in bundles, and carry them home to shadow their households.

It was so with the young husband on this particular occasion. The stream of business had taken an eddying whirl, and thrown his vessel backwards, instead of onwards, for a brief space; and, though it was still in the current, and gliding safely onwards again, the jar and disappointment had fretted his mind severely. There was no heart-warmth in the kiss he gave his wife, not because love had failed in any degree, but because he had let care overshadow love. He drew his arm around her; but she was conscious of a diminished pressure in that embracing arm.

"Are you not well?"

With what tender concern was the question asked!

"Very well."

He might be in body, but not in mind; that was plain; for his voice was far from being cheerful.

She played and sang his favorite pieces, hoping to restore, by the charm of music, brightness to his spirit. But she was conscious of only partial success. There was still a gravity in his manner never perceived before. At tea-time, she smiled upon him so sweetly across the table, and talked to him on such attractive themes, that the right expression returned to his countenance; and he looked as happy as she could desire.

From the tea-table, they returned to their pleasant parlor. And now the time had come for offering her gift, and receiving the coveted reward of glad surprise, followed by sweet kisses and loving words. Was she selfish? Did she think more of her reward than of the pleasure she would bestow? But that is questioning too closely.

"I will be back in a moment," she said; and, passing from the room, she went lightly up the stairs. Both tone and manner betrayed her secret, or rather the possession of a secret with which her husband was to be surprised. Scarcely had her loving face faded from before his eyes, when thought returned, with a single bound, to an unpleasant event of the day; and the waters of his spirit were again troubled. He had actually arisen, and crossed the floor once or twice, moved by a restless concern, when his wife came back with the dressing-gown and slippers. She was trying to force her countenance into a grave expression, to hold back the smiles that were continually striving to break in truant circles around her lips, when a single glance at her husband's face told her that the dark spirit, driven away by the exorcism of her love, had returned again to his bosom. He looked at her soberly, as she came forward.

"What are these?" he asked, almost coldly, repressing surprise, and affecting an ignorance, in regard to the beautiful present she held in her hands, that he did not feel.

"They are for you, dear. I made them."

"For me? Nonsense! What do I want with such jimcrackery? This is woman's wear. Do you think I would disfigure my feet with embroidered slippers, or dress up in a calico gown? Put them away, dear! Your husband is too much of a man to robe himself in gay colors, like a clown or actor." And he waved his hand with an air of contempt. There was a cold, sneering manner about him, partly affected and partly real—the real born of his uncomfortable state of mind. Yet he loved his sweet wife, and would not, of set purpose, have wounded her for the world.

This unexpected repulse—this cruel reception of her present, over which she had wrought, patiently, in golden hope for many days—this dashing to the earth her brimful cup of joy, just as it touched her lips, was more than the fond young wife could bear. To hide the tears that came rushing to her eyes, she turned away from her husband; and, to conceal the sobs she had no power to repress, she went almost hurriedly from the room; and, going back to the chamber from whence she had brought the present, she laid it away out of sight in a closet. Then covering her face with her hands, she sat down, and strove with herself to be calm. But the shadow was too deep—the heartache too heavy.

In a little while her husband followed her, and discovering, something to his surprise, that she was weeping, said, in a slightly reproving voice: "Why, bless me! not in tears! What a silly little puss you are! Why didn't you tell me you thought of making a dressing-gown and pair of slippers, and I would have vetoed the matter at once? You couldn't hire me to wear such flaunting things. Come back to the parlor"—he took hold of her arm, and lifted her from the chair—"and sing and play for me. 'The Dream Waltz,' or 'The Tremolo,' 'Dearest May,' or 'The Stilly Night' are worth more to me than forty dressing-gowns, or a cargo of embroidered slippers."

Almost by force, he led her back to the parlor, and placed her on the music-stool. He selected a favorite piece, and laid it before her. But tears were in her eyes; and she could not see a note. Over the keys her fingers passed in skillful touches; but, when she tried to take up the song, utterance failed; and sobs broke forth instead of words.

"How foolish!" said the husband, in a vexed tone. "I'm surprised at you!" And he turned from the piano, and walked across the room.

A little while the sad young wife remained where she was left thus alone, and in partial anger. Then, rising, she went slowly from the room—her husband not seeking to restrain her—and, going to her chamber, sat down in darkness.

The shadow which had been cast upon her spirit was very deep; and, though the hidden sun came out again right early, it was a long time before his beams had power to scatter the clouds that floated in love's horizon.

The shadows we cast! Father, husband, wife, sister, brother, son, neighbor—are we not all casting shadows daily, on some hearts that are pining for the sunlight of our faces? We have given you two pictures of life, true pictures, not as in a mirror, but in a kaleidoscope. In all their infinitely varied relations, men and women, selfishly, or thoughtlessly—from design, weakness, or ignorance—are casting their shadows upon hearts that are pining for sunlight. A word, a look, a tone, an act, will cast a shadow, and sadden a spirit for hours and days. Speak kindly, act kindly, be forgetters of self, and regardless of others, and you will cast but few shadows along the paths of life. The true gentleman is always tender of the feelings of others—always watchful, lest he wound unintentionally—always thinking, when with others, of their pleasure instead of his own. He casts but few shadows. Be gentlemen—ladies, or—in a word that includes all graces and excellences—Christians; for it is the Christian who casts fewest shadows of all.

XXVII.

GOOD DEEDS.

"He is paving the way to heaven by good deeds," said a lady. I bent my ear and listened.

"Unless it is very well paved, he will find progress in that direction exceedingly difficult." The reply fixed my attention.

"Are you not uncharitable?" remarked the first speaker. "Mr. Floyd does a great deal of good. I never go to him on an errand of benevolence, that he does not give me something."

"To buy paving-stones," was the quiet remark.

"Now, that is too bad!" said the other. "Give the man credit for what he does. By their fruit ye shall know them."

"God looks at the heart, not at the act. It isn't *what* a man does, that saves him, but *why* he does it. The quality is determined by the purposes, or ends of action, not by the outside work. Two men may do the same thing; yet, to one it may be a good act, and to the other an evil one."

"I don't know about that. A good deed is a good deed. By what process can you change its quality?"

"I thought," said the other, "that you would understand me clearly. The acts of the two men may benefit alike the objects; but, the actors will be blessed or cursed therein, according as their motives were good or evil."

"I am not just able," was replied, "to see how a good deed can be done from an evil purpose. For instance, I called on Mr. Floyd yesterday for a subscription to our Widows' Home, and he gave me ten dollars. That was a good act, and I can conceive of no prompting impulse but a good one."

The lady did not immediately reply; and I was about answering for her, when she said:

"If Mr. Floyd gave the ten dollars out of regard for the poor widows, then the act was a good act for him; but, if to appear benevolent, or to buy paving-stones for the road to heaven, then it was evil to him. For, in this latter case, love of the world and love of self, instead of neighborly love, ruled in his heart. And men only advance heavenward by the way of good aflections. He not only lost his money, but his reward. To the poor widows, the benefit was the same; but the donor's selfishness robbed him of his proper share."

"You go too deep for me," was answered to this. "And too deep, I fancy, for most people. Charity, the Bible tells us, covers a multitude of sins. And what is charity, but good deeds?"

"Charity is love of the neighbor, manifesting itself in good deeds," was the promptly-spoken reply.

"Very well; who will say that Mr. Floyd did not act from true neighborly love?"

"God only knows. The adjudication of the matter is between him and the human soul. If the motive which God sees, is right, the action will be good; if selfish, the action will be evil, so far as the actor is concerned."

"But, you judge Mr. Floyd."

"Did I? Well, there are many external signs by which we get an impression of a man's quality. Some men hang but a thin veil over their motives; while others, in their over anxiety for concealment, are constantly betraying themselves. Mr. Floyd is one of the most transparent men I know. He is constantly letting you see below the surface of his actions. The very air with which he hands you a contribution, betrays the lurking sentiment."

"Then," said the other, "he might as well shut up his bowels of compassion. If good deeds, such as he does, are not to be valid in heaven, he had better keep his own, and enjoy it to the full."

"Rather say, that he had better make the inside of his platter clean, also. Better cherish loving affections, and do genuine good from these, and so secure his share of benefits. What folly to halt in the way after this fashion—to be content with only the effigy of good deeds—to be satisfied to eat of the husks of men's extorted praise, instead of enjoying divine approval, and eating of heavenly food. As to selfishly enjoying what you call his own, that is impossible. The more he increases in worldly goods, the more wretched will he become, unless he uses them as a faithful steward of him who is the rightful owner of all. Like waters at rest, unused riches spoil, and curse their owners. So, if he will not give from the purest motives, still he had better give, for, in giving, he will find more delight than in withholding. Even the semblance of good deeds is better than no deeds at all.

The neighbor is benefited, and the selfish giver obtains some fleeting pleasure that stirs briefly along the surface of his life. It is next best to genuine charity."

"Judged by your standard, there is not much good done in the world," was answered.

"I fear," said the lady, "that there is less of genuine good done by any of us than we are inclined to give ourselves credit for. I know, too well, my own deficiencies."

"Which makes you sharp on others," the friend remarked, half playfully, half in earnest.

"Well retorted," was good humoredly answered, "and I accept the admonition; though, I do not by any means withdraw the main proposition, that the quality of our acts, in the sight of heaven, is determined by the indwelling motive. This, to me, is as apparent as the sun at noonday."

And the lady was right.

XXVIII.

RUINED.

"THE man is ruined—hopelessly ruined!"

The words startled me.

"So bad as that?" said the individual to whom the remark was made.

"Even so bad."

"Of whom are you speaking?" I ventured to ask.

"Of Jacob Atwood."

I started to my feet. He was one of my old, intimate, and long-tried friends.

"Ruined, did you say? That man ruined! Impossible!"

"There is no doubt of it. I received my information from those who have the best right to know."

"What has he done?" I asked, eagerly.

My question was received in silence, as if the meaning were not clearly apprehended.

"Is he a defaulter?"

"No." The answer showed surprise at my question.

"Has he betrayed an honorable trust reposed in him by his fellow-men?"

"No, sir; his integrity is without question. In all his public relations he was true as steel to principle."

"What then? Has he placed any portion of his property beyond the reach of creditors who have just claims upon him?"

"He has given up everything—even to the furniture of his house. Not a dollar has been retained, and he goes forth into the world a ruined man."

"Oh no," said I, speaking out warmly. "Not in any sense a ruined *man*. The merchant may be ruined, but, thank God! the *man* is whole."

The little company looked at me, for a moment or two, half in surprise.

"The man is all right," I went on. "Only the scaffolding on which the workmen stood who were building up his character, has fallen. Erect, calm, noble, half-divine, he stands, now, in the sunshine and in the storm. Around his majestic brow the clouds may gather; upon it the tempests may beat; but he is immovable in his great integrity."

Some smiled at my enthusiasm. To them there was nothing of the moral sublime in a ruined merchant. Others looked a little more thoughtful than before; and one said feebly:

"There is something in that."

Something in that! I should think there was.

It was the first intelligence I had received of my friend's worldly misfortunes, and it grieved me. In the evening I went to see Jacob Atwood. The windows of the elegant residence where he had lived for years were closed. I looked up at the house—it had a deserted aspect. I rung the bell; no one answered my summons.

I could not repress the feeling of sadness that came over me. The trial must have been severe even for a brave heart like his.

"I must find him," said I. And I did find him; but far away from the neighborhood where merchant princes had their palace-homes. The house into which he had retired with his family looked small, and mean, and comfortless, in comparison with the elegant abode from which he had removed. I rung and was admitted. The parlor into which I was shown was a small room, and the furniture not much better than we often see in the houses of well-to-do mechanics, or clerks on moderate salaries. But everything was in order, and scrupulously neat.

I had made only a hurried observation, when Mr. Atwood entered. He looked something careworn—his face was paler than when I last saw him, his eyes a little duller, his smile less cheerful. The marks of trial and suffering were plainly visible. It would have been almost a miracle had it been otherwise. But he did not exhibit the aspect of a ruined man. He grasped my hand warmly, and said it was pleasant to look into the face of an old friend. I offered him words of sympathy.

"The worst is over," he answered, with manly cheerfulness, "and nothing is lost which may not be regained. I have found the bottom, know where I am, and there is strength enough left in me to stand up securely amid the rushing waters. The best of all is, my property, which has been apportioned to my creditors, will pay every debt. That gives my heart its lightest pulsations."

"I heard that you were *ruined*," said I, as we sat talking together; "but I find that the man is whole. Not a principle invaded by the enemy—not a moral sentiment lost—not a jewel in the crown of honor missing."

He took my hand, and grasping it hard, looked into my face steadily for some moments. Then, in a subdued voice, he made answer—

"I trust that it is even so, my friend. But there were seasons in the worse than Egpytian night through which I have passed, when the tempter's power seemed about to crush me. For myself I cared little; for my wife and children everything. The thought of seeing them go out from the pleasant home I had provided for them, and step down, far down to a lower level in the social grade, half distracted me for a time. For them I would have braved everything but an evil deed, that is sin against God. I could not bow to that. And so I passed the fiery ordeal, and have come out through a more than human strength, I trust, a better man. No, no, no, my friend. I am not ruined. I have lost my fortune, but not my integrity."

And so the man stood firm. It was not in the power of any commercial disaster to ruin him. The storm raged furiously; the waves beat madly against him; but he stood immovable, for his feet were upon solid rock.

XXIX.

PROVIDENCE.

"It is very dark, but I am trying to put my trust in Providence," said a merchant, as he sat one evening in conversation with the minister of his church, who had called to spend in an hour with him. "Men are falling around me, like soldiers in battle; yet I am still on my feet, moving forwards, though not seeing the way clear before me for a single week. The Lord has helped me hitherto, when the way was as difficult as it is now; and though I tremble, I still look up in hope."

The minister listened, but did not answer at once. He saw that in the mind of his parishioner God's providence went scarcely beyond the things of natural life.

"God is an infinite and eternal being, Mr. Harding," he said, letting his voice dwell, as he spoke, on the words "infinite" and "eternal."

The merchant lifted his eyes to the minister's face, and looked at him earnestly.

"His ends, therefore, must be infinite and eternal, and, in no case, limited to time."

"I am not sure that I take your meaning," said the merchant, with a half-bewildered air.

"The providence of God, as I understand it," said the spiritual instructor, "regards, as of first and highest importance, the salvation of our souls from evil, and things temporal as always subordinated. If prosperity will in any degree help a man towards heaven, or prevent him from sinking to a lower place in hell, then God permits him to prosper in the world; and if adversity is needed for the same purpose, then adversity will come in spite of human prudence. It is always man's spiritual good that determines the action of Providence, not his natural enjoyment."

An expression of blank fear settled in the merchant's face. This was to him a new and alarming proposition; for though what is called a pious man, that is one strictly observant of all church ordinances, and exteriorly devout, his heart was in the good things of this world more than in the heavenly things of the next. He took delight in laying up treasure on the earth; and spent much care in guarding it from moth, and rust, and thieves. But in the work of laying up treasure for Heaven, he had really accomplished but little; for his heart was not in this work. There was no genuine love in his Sabbath worship, no spiritual affection in his morning prayers. His religion was a kind of bribe thrown to Heaven; a concession made for temporal security and final safety. No wonder that this new doctrine startled him.

"If your reading of the doctrine of Providence be correct," said he, after musing for a while, and speaking in a husky tone of voice, "I don't see much to encourage me in this day of sore trouble."

"Why not?"

"My spiritual well-being may"——

The merchant paused, unwilling to clothe his thoughts in words.

"Require the discipline of adversity," said the minister, concluding the sentence for him.

There was a sign of anguish in the merchant's face—of anguish mingled with fear.

"You bring me no comfort," said he. "This is a hard doctrine."

"What shall it profit a man if he gain the whole

world and lose his own soul?" The minister spoke almost solemnly.

"I do not want the whole world," answered the merchant, as if pleading for his earthly goods: "I am not covetous for great riches. My heart is not set on gold. I am content with what I have."

"But would you not be willing to part with all your possessions, if in doing so you could secure eternal felicities?" asked the minister.

"I don't see how my being crushed down now, and being overwhelmed with ruin, is going to advance my spiritual welfare," replied the merchant, visibly excited.

"My dear brother," said the minister, "God's ways are not as our ways. He is infinitely wise and infinitely good, and therefore cannot err nor be unkind. He will permit nothing to happen to you or to me that is not designed to secure in some way our eternal well-being. Let us not be like short-sighted and rebellious children, who resist the discipline of their wiser parents. All souls are alike precious in his eyes; and he cares for all with an infinite love. Your neighbor, whose fortunes fell, shattered into a thousand fragments, last week, is equal with you in the eyes of God; and he regarded him in love when he permitted swift-footed misfortune to overtake him. Your neighbor, on the other side, fell also; but he was not without the sphere of Providence, nor was the visitation in anger, but in tenderest mercy. It may be that you will pass safely through; but your standing or falling will depend on the security of your eternal interest. Whatever is best for the elevation of your soul towards Heaven will occur. Your Father loves you too well to permit temporal and perishing things to rule over and destroy what is spiritual. Let me pray you to submit yourself, as an obedient child, to the will of God. Work faithfully, vigorously; do all in your power, by honorable means, to sustain yourself, and leave the result to Him in whose hands we are as clay in the hands of the potter. Whatever comes will be for the best; and you will live to see the day when you can look back and bless God even for misfortune, should it shadow your path of life."

As the minister was retiring, after having in vain striven to lift the merchant's mind upwards into a clear perception of the true doctrine of Providence, the latter said to him, in a depressed tone of voice:

"You have taken away my confidence. I was

trusting in Providence, and hoping for a right issue, even in the face of most discouraging signs: I was not faithless, but believing; now, doubt and gloom overshadow me. My strength is gone. I have no heart to struggle in the meshes that fetter my limbs."

"There is no night that does not precede a morning," replied the minister, as he held the merchant's hand tightly in his own. "In every death is involved a resurrection. Night shadows the heart with gloomy fears, and death comes with pain. But the morning breaks in joy, and, through the resurrection, we rise into a superior life. Do not shrink, then, from the dark night of misfortune, if it is to come, nor from the death of natural affections; for without the latter it is impossible for spiritual life to be born."

Then, with a strong pressure on the merchant's hand, he turned from him and took his way homeward.

A sleepless night did the merchant pass. It was indeed true that the minister's words had taken away his confidence. He could trust in Providence for natural good no longer. The truth had reached down and taken hold of his convictions. He saw that eternal ends were first and highest; and that Divine Wisdom could not have regard to natural things, except as servants of the spiritual. He saw, too, that, in the eyes of God, he was only his brother's equal; and that all souls were alike precious.

"Hundreds of men as good as I am, and hundreds who are far better, have been stricken down in this wide-reaching calamity," he said to himself, as he pondered the new aspect of things; "and can I say that the same hard discipline is not required for me? No, no, I cannot—I cannot."

Drearily broke the morning; and the merchant went forth to his business with a heart heavily oppressed; for he was not strong enough to accept the higher truth which had forced itself upon his rational convictions. He was not yet willing to give up his natural good, that spiritual life might be born. Reason had become clear, but the heart was weak. There was nothing to encourage him in the business of the day. New failures had taken place, and new losses shaken the house in which he was a partner to the very foundations. The most hopeful of all his partners began to talk despondingly.

Two days more of struggle and loss went by; and then the partners met alone, in the evening, at their store, to take counsel of one another, and to ascertain, as accurately as possible, their real condition and prospects. The issue was of the most disheartening character; for a hurried examination of their books showed that losses had already swept away their entire capital, and that if the ratio of losses among their entire list of customers was maintained, they would not have assets sufficient to pay forty cents in the dollar of their debts.

And so that terrible calamity, so dreaded by all honorable men and so hard to accept—commercial failure—was at the merchant's door, and he saw no way of escape.

"We may save something from the wreck," suggested one of the partners.

"How?" was the eager question.

The means were proposed by which, in compounding with creditors, each partner might retain enough to get into business again.

"We can do it with the greatest ease, and none be the wiser for it," said the partner. "I can't see that we are called upon wholly to beggar ourselves. This disaster is not from any fault of our own. If we could get in what is due, we could pay dollar for dollar, and have a large surplus. Why, then, should we be made the victims of circumstances? I believe that I am as honest as any man living; but there are necessities which reach beyond human control."

Then followed a silent pondering of the plan suggested; and then the other partner simply said,

"It might be done."

"It can and must be done," said the one who had opened the matter. He spoke with energy. "Desperate diseases require desperate remedies. I, for one, have no notion of being driven to the wall if I can help it; of tamely submitting, when a manful struggle will save me from total wreck."

"The plan involves subterfuge," our merchant, the senior partner, remarked.

There was no reply.

"And concealment."

"No great harm in that. We are not called upon to exhibit every aspect of our affairs to the world," was answered.

"And mercantile dishonor."

"You are too scrupulous, sir," replied the advocate of the plan—"altogether too scrupulous. Mercantile honor may become ideal and heroic. Remember that we owe something to ourselves and to our families. Self-sacrifice is not the genius of to-day. We are not required to throw ourselves under the crushing wheels of every Juggernaut-car a contracted public opinion may send rumbling through our streets. No, no; it were folly to let events cripple us hopelessly, while there are time and means to avert such a direful calamity. Desperate diseases, as I have said before, require desperate remedies. Let us act promptly, and thus save ourselves from the worst."

The merchant was tempted by the specious plan, and urged to its adoption by the fearful consequences that impended. But the temptation proved his quality.

"There is only one right course for us," he said, in answer to his partner's earnest attempt to draw him over—and he spoke in a sad but firm voice —"and that is the straightforward, honorable, honest one of making a fair exhibit. Anything short of this may seem to involve a present good; but, depend upon it, evils worse than we now dread will be sure to meet us in the future, if we yield to dishonest suggestions."

But the partners were against him, and the contest proved long and angry. He did not yield, however; and without unanimous action no scheme of fraud could be consummated

A little while longer the struggle continued; then the house went down with a crash, and only with their lives, so to speak, did the partners escape from the ruins. Nothing was saved from the wreck of their fortunes. The creditors took everything, under a general assignment. The senior partner, in whom the highest confidence was placed, they offered to retain, for the purpose of settling up the business under the assignee; and the offer was gladly accepted, as it gave at least a temporary provision for his family.

Two months after the disastrous event, this conversation took place between the minister and his old parishioner. The minister had called to see him in his humble home. He was met with a smile on the paler face of the reduced merchant, and with a warm grasp of his hand.

" Cast down, but not forsaken," said the minister, with an answering smile, and in a tone of cheerful encouragement, as he returned the earnest pressure.

"No, not forsaken," replied the merchant, with feeling. "Not forsaken, but sustained. I have passed through deep waters; the floods roared about me; but I was not overwhelmed. I was tried in the furnace, but the fires have not consumed me. If it is night, the whole firmament is glittering with stars."

"Were you really happier before your misfortune, than you have been since?" inquired the minister. The merchant was thoughtful for a little while. He then answered—

"It may sound strangely, but I have since had states of mind that were nearer happiness than anything enjoyed before. I am more tranquil, and patient, and resigned to the will of Providence. I can look deeper into my own heart, and understand its impulses better. My soul more clearly appreciates the higher value of spiritual and eternal things. Ah, sir, I now see clearly that better truth in regard to Providence, which you so vainly sought to make me comprehend a few short weeks ago. How blind and rebellious I was! How dim had my vision become, through love of the world. But, God let misfortune fall upon me for my good; and the hard discipline is doing its work. When the crisis came, I found the tempter at hand in my partners, who suggested that we should secure something for ourselves. But, I was able to resist; and in the most painful ordeal of my whole life, to maintain an undeviating integrity. How many, many times since, have I thanked God for the strength he gave me in that hour of darkness and sore trial."

"Then, you are really happier than before," said the minister.

"I am more peaceful, more trusting, more desirous of spiritual attainments."

"If more peaceful, then happier. God has permitted these natural misfortunes to come in blessing, not in wrath. And whenever prosperity can be given without danger to your soul, it will come again. Our Heavenly Father gives to his children of natural good, all that they can receive without endangering their eternal welfare, and takes it from them, whenever the discipline of adversity is needed."

"It is plain to me, now, that I needed the discipline," said the merchant. "Without it, I never could have risen into my present views of providence—never could have seen, I fear, that all natural events are but a series of effects bearing upon spiritual and eternal things as ends in the Divine economy. And without such a perception, what dark, ignorant, groping creatures we are. How full of mystery is everything around us. How shadowed by doubts and vague questionings the uncertain way we tread with halting feet."

"Enough," said the minister. "The lesson God designed to teach, you have quickly learned. Adversity has come as a priceless blessing; for you have exchanged gold for spiritual wisdom—the excitement of natural life, for heavenly tranquillity—a restless love of gain for divine repose. Ah, my brother; our Father in Heaven is better to his children than all their fears."

XXX.

THE WAGES OF THE POOR.

"How much is it?" asked the lady, as she drew out her purse, and poured from it into her hand a little pile of silver coins. Before her stood a pale, poorly-dressed, weary-looking woman.

"Seventy-five cents, ma'am," was answered.

"Seventy-five cents!" the lady's voice expressed surprise. "No, no, Mary; I can't give that price for three quarters of a day's work. You did not come until after nine o'clock, remember. If you want full wages, you must do full work. Sixty-two is all that I can give you."

"I'll have to take it, then," said the woman, rather sadly. "My little Eddy was sick, and I couldn't get away as early as I wanted to this morning; but I have worked hard all day to make up. I think I have earned it."

"No doubt of that in the world, Mary," broke out the cheerful voice of the lady's husband, who was sitting in the room; "and here's twenty-five cents extra to my wife's sixty-two. She's a prudent woman, and tries to be careful of my money; but she's over particular to-night, it strikes me. Buy Eddy something that he will like, as you go home, out of the odd shilling, and say that I sent it to him."

"Oh, thank you! thank you, sir!" exclaimed the poor working woman, a sudden light breaking over her face. "You are very good!"

Then she retired, and husband and wife were left alone.

"That wasn't just right, Mr. Lawson," said the lady, speaking seriously.

"I know it wasn't, and therefore I corrected your error at once," replied Mr. Lawson, as coolly as if he had not really understood the meaning of his wife's remark.

"It wasn't right, I mean, for you to interfere as you did just now. What's the use of my trying to be economical if you circumvent me in this way? Mary was not entitled to full day's wages."

"I think she was," said the husband.

"How will you make that out? Let me see your calculation."

"I can make it out in several ways; can give you the figures, and prove the sum. First, then, she alleges that she worked hard all day to make up, and thinks she really earned a full day's wages. There's the sum worked out clearly. Now, as to proof of the result, I would first offer humanity; next, the woman's loss of strength in a day's hard toil, for she looked so pale and weary that the very sight of her gave me pain; next, her poverty; for the mother of three children, who goes out to do washing and house-cleaning in order to get bread for them, must be very poor; next, a sick child, who may need medicine, or some daintier food than usual. Do you want further proof that she was entitled to receive full pay for a day's work?"

There was a change in the countenance of Mrs. Lawson before her husband had finished these sentences.

"Perhaps you are right," she said. "These poor women do work very hard for what they get, and I often feel sorry for them. I'm glad, at least, that you gave Mary the extra quarter. Still, Mr. Lawson, we cannot afford to overpay people who work for us if they are poor. A shilling here, and a shilling there, repeated over and over again, daily, will amount to a serious item in the year; and, when the shillings are not really earned, will prove, in most cases, but incentives to idleness."

"The other side of the case, my dear," answered Mr. Lawson, "and very well stated. But let us be careful in our transactions with these poor people, that we do not withhold the shilling actually due in our over-nice calculations as to the time they may be in our service. At best, their labor is poorly compensated. They toil hard, very hard, for the small sum they ask for services rendered; and we can always better afford to give ten extra shillings in a week than they can afford to lose one. Let us not increase our comforts, or add to our possessions, at their cost; but let them be rather objects of our care, sympathy, and protection. The Psalmist says: 'Blessed is he that considereth the poor; the Lord will deliver him in time of trouble.' There is a vast deal more to gain than to lose, I take it, in concessions to these humbler children of our common Father."

"Mrs. Lawson sighed as her husband ceased speaking. His words brought out from her memory more than a single instance where she had paid to the extremely poor, who rendered her service for hire, less than the price demanded, under the allegation of an excessive charge for work. In her over-carefulness about what was her own, she had withheld pennies, sixpences, and shillings, which really added nothing to her comforts, but diminished the comforts of the poor. Coming back upon her now, these memories troubled her.

"I am afraid," she remarked, looking with a sober aspect, into her husband's face, "that I have not been altogether just in these matters. But you have set me right. I will try to be more considerate and more humane in future. I did not, really, perceive the meaning of what Mary said about having worked hard all day to make up for loss of time, nor feel the allusion to the sick child, or I could not have had the heart to withhold that shilling. Our very thoughtlessness sometimes leads us into wrong."

"There is, as a general thing," remarked Mr. Lawson, "a disposition to reduce still lower than their present low rate, the wages of the extremely poor, especially the poor who earn their living among housekeepers. The seamstress, the washerwoman, and the day's-work woman, all have to toil very hard for their meagre wages; and the disposition is to take off the sixpences and the shillings whenever there is an excuse for doing so, instead of a generous concession in their favor. I remember an instance of this kind which happened to fall under my observation some years ago. A lady was quite indignant at what she was pleased to call an attempt at extortion on the part of a poor woman, who had been cleaning house for her, in charging her sixty-two cents a-day, instead of fifty. The poor woman said that she always received sixty-two cents, and the lady declared that she never paid but fifty cents, and would not exceed that sum in the present case. And fifty cents was all she did pay. I noticed the dejection of the poor, wronged creature, as she retired from the house, and could not but feel a sense of indignation, which was in no degree lessened when I saw the lady hand the shilling she had gained by oppression to an idle daughter, and heard her say, 'Here, Jenny, is a shilling I have saved. You can treat yourself to an ice cream to-morrow!'"

"Are you really in earnest?" said Mrs. Lawson, looking at her husband with a doubting air.

"What I have told you is literally true."

"Doesn't it seem impossible?"

"It is wicked and disgraceful. But such things are of daily occurrence," replied Mr. Lawson. "There is a better way, however, and a more Christian spirit. Let us walk in this way; let us encourage this spirit. If we change the wages of the poor in anything, let it be to increase, not diminish them; for Heaven knows they have been reduced enough already!"

XXXI.

THE DREAM-WARNING.

"WILL you discount this note for me?"

The question was asked by a merchant, in the office of a private banker, a man of large fortune, who had retired from business, and now used his capital for discounting instead of in trade.

The shrewd money-lender took the note, and after examining the face, handed it back, with a shake of the head, and a very firm compression of his mouth.

"It is A number one," said the merchant, with almost an amused smile, at the severe prudence of the money-lender.

"I have no question as to that," was replied. "If I were in business, I should not hesitate to sell the firm to any reasonable extent."

"Why, then, will you not buy their note?"

A pleasant light came into the money-lender's

face. He looked shrewd, knowing, and very self-complacent.

"I was in market the other day," said he, "and as I stood buying some fruit at a woman's stall, a man, in going by, was crowded against a basket standing thereon, which fell to the pavement. It was nearly filled with eggs, more than two-thirds of which were broken. 'Ah, my good woman,' said I, 'the old error of too many eggs in one basket. If you had placed them in two or three baskets, instead of one, this general wreck would never have occurred.' In my business, sir," continued the money-lender, "I never commit the error of this market-woman. I never place too many eggs in one basket. Do you understand me?"

"I believe so," replied the merchant. "You already have enough of this paper."

"Just as much as I intend buying. When some of it is taken up, I will make room for more. There are fixed laws, sir, that govern me in this business, and I never depart from them.

"Good morning," said the merchant, smiling. "I hope you will never get too many eggs in one basket."

"No fear of that. If a basket is upset, and the eggs in it broken, I shall be able to bear the loss."

The merchant withdrew, and the money-lender turned over in his mind the word just spoken, and felt self-complimented at his wise caution. "No—no"—he repeated over and over again. "They cannot tempt me to place too many eggs in one basket. I am too old and prudent for that."

This figure of speech seemed to please the money-lender, and he used it a number of times during the day, in declining good business paper that was offered.

"Have I put too many eggs in one basket, to-day?" he asked of himself, as he sat alone during the evening that followed, counting up, mentally, his gains, and looking with a feeling of pleasure, at the unusually large aggregate. "Let me see? That last note of L—— & O——'s came very near to a violation of the rule. There are quite enough eggs in that basket. I must not venture another one. But the temptation of two per cent. was hardly to be resisted on such paper, which all regard as gilt-edged."

It was now over five years since our money-lender withdrew from productive trade, and narrowed down his intellect and his efforts to the simple business of buying paper, which the holders were unable to get done in bank. During that period he had added largely to his wealth; while his desire for accumulation had grown stronger, and manifested itself in a more eager reaching out after, and drawing in of the gold that perishes. As a merchant, he had been liberal, generous, kind-hearted; and all men spoke of him as such. But the work of mere money-getting, outside of any productive use in society, had brought the interiors of his mind into new associations; and his heart was steadily hardening. Every day the circle of his thoughts narrowed itself; every day his heart stooped lower and lower in adoration before the miser's god. Others saw the change—spoke of it, and regretted it. But, as he grew richer and richer, and the worshippers of riches bent to him in flattery, he imagined himself to be growing better.

"Too many eggs in one basket," he repeated to himself, as he sat musing in his luxurious easy-chair; never for once thinking of the young merchant, without bank credit, more than two-thirds of whose profits on a sale of five hundred dollars he had clipped off a six months' note that day; a note as good as any he had bought during the past week.

"Too many eggs in one basket! No—no. I am too shrewd for that!" Drowsily was this murmured, as he laid his head back among the cushions. His next consciousness was in another world. He dreamed that he had passed through the dark portal of eternity, and that to him the judgment from the Book of his Life had come—a judgment that was to reveal his true state, and fix his everlasting habitation with those who loved the neighbor as themselves; or with those who loved and cared only for themselves. He did not find himself in the presence of an august, Divine Judge, but in a large chamber, with translucent walls and ceiling, where were gathered a small assemblage of people, to the centre of which he was led by one who seemed to possess a singular power over him. Here, seated, and a little elevated above the rest, were two beings—one with a countenance of heavenly beauty, and the other with a face the cruel expression of which caused a shudder to go thrilling to his heart. A book lay open before them, and he knew it to be the Book of his Life, wherein were written every purpose of his heart, with every act and deed. The money-lender had come to judgment.

With a hopeful countenance the angel began turning the leaves of the book, upon which both her eyes, and that of the demon were fixed with an earnest gaze. The period of childhood showed a fair and hopeful record. The tender, merciful, loving impressions made upon the heart of her child by a wise and good mother, who looked forward to a meeting with her son in heaven, were everywhere visible. The budding soil gave a fair promise for the fruit and flower.

Early manhood's record was also full of encouragement. There was an eager looking forwards into life, and an earnest will towards success. But, united with this, were generous purposes towards others, and great humanitary schemes to be wrought out for the world's good, when the money-power to work should come within his grasp. There were light and hope in the angel's face, as page after page of the book was turned; while the demon sat dark and scowling.

The middle period showed less fairly, as to the

ends of life—and it was into these that the angel and the demon looked most narrowly. The act was never judged of as it stood alone—it was by the motive that its quality was determined.

A gentle sadness began to shadow the angel's beautiful countenance, while dimly seen in the demon's face was the light of triumph. Many acts of benevolence; many words of good counsel to others; many declarations of noble, generous, unselfish purposes were written down; but they were seen as deeds with selfish ends for prompters, and words that were only from the "teeth outwards." More and more, as wealth rolled into the merchant's coffers, and he gained a higher and higher place in the good opinions of men, did he bury his thoughts in selfish purposes, and put forth his strength for himself alone, as if he were the chiefest thing in God's creation. His name was on the subscription papers, for charitable uses, to a large amount; but, when the angel and the demon went behind the record, what did they find? A generous desire to benefit the suffering, or help the weak? Alas, no! They saw, instead, an extorted benevolence, in most instances, done for the eyes of men, and succeeded by a self-complacent gratulation, in the loss of so much of his dearly-loved gains, that "charity covers a multitude of sins!"

Sadder and sadder grew the angel's face; brighter and brighter, with an evil triumph, the face of the demon.

At last came the closing years of life, when the useful merchant sunk down into the eager money-lender. Previous to this, gleams of better purposes would sometimes throw a hopeful warmth over a page, and lighten the saddening angel's face. But the record now had in it little of variation, and no passages of light. Desire moved on in an even current, and thought had free course under the pressure of desire. There was the one desire to get money, and the one thought about the surest means. The face of a man—the form of a man—the step of a man—but quickened his avaricious impulses. He was a great tumor, absorbing the rich blood of trade, and growing larger and larger, as healthy, working organs in the man of society became weaker from impaired vitality. Gold had become the god before whom he bowed down in daily adoration. He loved naught else; and though, from a lingering desire to appear well in the eyes of his fellow-men, he still performed some apparent good acts; yet, in every such act, there was the effort to compass a worldly advantage that marred the record in his book of life. Thus, for instance, he had given liberally to the erection of churches, but only when they were to be located near his property, the value of which would be improved thereby far beyond the sum of his subscription.

As the last page of the book was turned, the angel breathed a deep sigh, and faded from the money-lender's vision!

"Too many eggs in one basket!" said the demon, in a voice of triumph, as he bent his malignant face so close that his hot breath almost suffocated the terrified money-lender, who started into wakeful life as he felt himself clutched by the demon's vice-like hands. Some moments passed before his wildly-throbbing heart calmed itself down to its wonted even pulsations.

"Only a dream—a foolish dream!" he said to himself, as he vainly tried to rise above the depressed state of feeling which the mercifully sent vision had left behind.

But conscience told him that it was more than a dream, and that, while in all worldly prudence he was wisely careful not to get too many eggs in a single basket, in matters of eternal interest he had one basket only, and in that the price of his soul was resting. He shuddered as the thought fixed his mind, and overwhelmed all his convictions.

"What shall it profit a man if he gain the whole world and lose his own soul? or what will a man give in exchange for his soul?"

It seemed like the voice of his mother, speaking back to him from the years of childhood.

"God help me!" he said, with a shudder. "I am not in the right path!"

Did he go back to his eager money-getting and money-lending? We know not. The dream was sent in mercy, and let us hope that it wrought upon him its high and holy mission.

XXXII.

IN THE WORKSHOP.

"You are not going to put in that piece of wood, Richard," said one workman to another.

"Yes, I am. No one will be the wiser for it," was answered.

"But some one may be wronged by it."

"No very serious wrong. The worst that can happen will be a rickety drawer."

"But, Richard, if you will take the trouble to go up into the third story, and select a better seasoned piece of wood, you will then be able to furnish a drawer that will always run smoothly."

"I am not going to take that trouble. Mrs. Thompson would be very far from putting herself out as much for me."

"It doesn't strike me that you have anything to do with Mrs. Thompson's disposition towards you in the case. It is a simple question of right and wrong. You are at work on a bureau, for which she has agreed to pay our employer a certain price. The understanding is, of course, that the wood and workmanship are to be of good quality. Now, if you put in that piece of wood, you will wrong both Mrs. Thompson and our employer. She will receive a defective, troublesome article, and he will be injured in his business—for Mrs. Thompson would hardly engage him to make another piece of furniture after finding herself deceived. Your doing this thing, Richard, is, according to my notion, a violation of Christian charity."

"I don't see that Christian charity has anything to do in the matter. Mrs. Thompson crowded down in the price, and I am not too well paid for my part of the work. So, you see, I can't afford to be hunting about after seasoned wood. This piece comes nicely to my hand, and I am going to use it."

"I have nothing more to say," replied the fellow-workman, "except to repeat my judgment of your act, and call it a violation of Christian charity. Our praying, singing, and Bible-reading, Richard, will not help us heavenwards unless we are just between man and man. The Christian profession is nothing without the Christian life. Our religion, in order to change us radically, must descend into all our commonest duties. It belongs as much to the shop as to the family, and as much to the family as to the sanctuary. If you put in that piece of wood, knowing, as you do, that it will render the bureau you are making permanently defective, you will hurt your own soul."

"Don't trouble yourself about my soul," was the rather short reply. "I will take good care of that. If you hadn't said so much about it—magnifying a molehill into a mountain—I might have selected a better piece of wood; but this shall go in now. I'll risk the consequences."

"The risk may be greater than you imagine. It generally is in all such cases," was the grave reply.

And here the remonstrance closed. Richard Wheeler, the journeyman cabinet-maker, worked in the unseasoned piece of wood, and went on to finish the bureau, which was sent home at the time agreed upon, and the price paid. We do not know whether the suggestions of his fellow-workman remained with him or not, or whether the unseasoned piece of wood troubled, in any wise, his conscience.

Time passed on. The bureau, which had been placed in the chamber of Mrs. Thompson, gave good satisfaction for a time; but the unseasoned piece of wood failed at length to do its proper duty, and the drawer began halting in its work. The disproportionate shrinkage of one side of the drawer bent all the parts out of line, and so the opening and closing thereof was always attended with more or less difficulty.

Richard, the journeyman who made the bureau, was in the wareroom one day, when Mrs. Thompson came in, and, with some warmth of manner, said to his employer—

"I don't think you have dealt fairly by me in that bureau, Mr. Cartwright."

"Rather a grave charge, Mrs. Thompson," replied the cabinet-maker. "Why do you say so?"

"You hav'n't made it of properly seasoned wood, a thing for which I particularly stipulated," said the lady.

"I beg your pardon, madam"—Mr. Cartwright spoke with visible indignation—"the wood *was* properly seasoned."

"And I say that it was not." Mrs. Thompson was growing excited. "Why, there's one drawer in particular so all awry from shrinkage in some parts of it that it requires more humoring to get it in and out than I have the patience to give. I'm tempted some days to have the whole thing pitched into the street. It would be a disgrace to the poorest cabinet-tmaker in the city!"

This was rather more than Mr. Cartwright could bear. He lost temper entirely, and gave Mrs. Thompson so bluff a reply, that she went off in a passion, threatening, as she did so, to warn all her friends against the cabinet-maker's establishment.

"Richard made a hasty retreat from the wareroom to the workshop. His state of mind was not one to be envied. Here was the evil fruit of his wrong act; and what a monstrous production from so small a seed! He had not only been unjust to Mrs. Thompson, but had seriously injured his employer; for it was plain, that custom would be diverted from his establishment through his improper act.

The journeyman carried a sober heart home with him at the close of that day. His fellow-workman, the one who had remonstrated with him about putting into the bureau drawer an unseasoned piece of wood, called for him after supper to go with him to a religious meeting; but Richard declined. For the first time, he saw clearly the want of agreement between his conduct, in this particular, and that which was demanded by the divine law of justice from man to man.

"Come!" urged his fellow-workman.

But Richard said, "No, not to-night," in such a resolute way, that he was left to himself. He passed the evening in a very unhappy frame of mind.

On the next Sunday, he attended church as usual. He was still troubled in his thoughts by what had occurred. Singularly enough, it seemed to him, that almost every sentence spoken by the preacher had a more or less remote application to himself. Every proposition was a mirror in which he could see his own distorted image. But the closing portions of the sermon, when the preacher gathered his generalities together, and condensed them into specific applications, smote him with humiliating convictions of wrong.

"No man can be a Christian," said the minister, "who is not faithful in his common, daily-life pursuits. The judge must administer justice from equity, and not from favor or the lure of bribes; the physician must regard the life and health of his patient above all other considerations; the merchant must deal justly, and the mechanic execute his work in all things faithfully. It will not answer to disregard these things. My brother"—and the minister warmed in his manner, as he leaned over the pulpit and looked, as it seemed, to Richard, directly into the pew where he sat—"do not hope to reach heaven by the old way. You must walk in another, and narrower, road. Let us suppose you are a workman. Now, what is Christianity in the workshop? You must take it with you there, remember. You cannot leave it behind you, go where you will; for it is no loosely-fitting garment, but an element of life. Yes, you must take it with you into the workshop, my brother. Not as the Bible, in your hand; nor as hymns, to make the air melodious; nor as pious talk with fellow-workmen. No, no. Workshop Christianity consists in a religious fidelity to your employer and his customers. If you neglect or slight the work you are paid to perform, you commit sin: you are irreligious, and your pious acts will go for nothing."

What further the preacher said, Richard knew not. He passed, in his application, to the trader, manufacturer, and the various professions in life; but his thought was bound by the artisan's duty.

"A sad thing happened this morning," said Richard's wife, on his returning from work one day in the following week. "Mrs. Thompson broke a blood-vessel, and now lies very ill. The doctors have but little hope of her recovery."

"How did that happen?" asked the mechanic, with a sudden sense of uneasiness.

"She was trying to push in a drawer that didn't run smoothly, when it caught, and the jar, I believe, caused the blood-vessel to break. It was a bureau drawer. What's the matter, Richard? You look pale. Are you sick?"

His wife spoke these last sentences in a tone of anxiety.

"I don't feel very well," he answered; "but it's nothing of consequence. Did you say that she was thought to be in danger?"

"Yes. She lies very low."

Richard turned his face away. When supper was placed before him, he tried to eat, in order that his wife might not see how deeply he was troubled; but only a few mouthfuls passed his lips. Silent, and apart from the family, he sat during the evening; and the night which followed was, for the most part, sleepless.

On his way to work next morning, Richard went past the dwelling of Mrs. Thompson. He almost feared to look at the house when he came in sight, lest death-signs on the door should give the fatal intelligence of her dissolution. He breathed more freely when he saw that all remained as usual. So anxious was he, that he stopped and made inquiry as to her condition.

"Something better." How the words made his heart leap.

"Is she out of danger?" he asked, almost tremblingly.

"Oh, no; but the doctor speaks encouragingly."

Richard went on his way. At night, as he returned homewards, he called to inquire again.

"She is no worse." This was all the comfort he received; and on this he passed another restless night.

"If she dies, am I not her murderer?" This was the thought that troubled him so deeply, and made him so anxious about the life of Mrs. Thomp son. It was more than a week before all danger seemed passed; and then the unhappy workman breathed more freely. How the thin, white face, and feeble steps, of Mrs. Thompson rebuked him, a month afterwards, as he met her one day in the street! He could not rest after that, until he had obtained possession of the bureau drawer, and adjusted it so accurately to its place, that it might be moved in and out by the hand of a child. In doing this, he took care to remove the defective piece of wood.

"Why have *you* done this?" It was the sudden question of Mrs. Thompson, as Richard, having made all right, was about leaving the house.

He was confused.

"I did not send for you to do this."

The dark eyes of Mrs. Thompson looked out from their hollow sockets upon the almost startled workman.

"There was an unseasoned piece of wood in that drawer," said Richard, speaking with as much calmness as he could assume. "I wrongly placed it there, and I alone am to blame. Mr. Cartwright believed that every part of the work was of seasoned wood, according to agreement. He never meant to wrong you. He is an honest man. Oh, ma'am! if you can forgive me, do so; for, since the accident to yourself, I have been one of the most wretched of men."

"I can do no less than forgive," answered the lady, gravely; "and I hope God will forgive also; for you have been the agent of a great wrong."

The journeyman cabinet-maker retired, with a lesson in his heart that it was impossible ever to forget. After that, he tried to bring his religion into the workshop; and he was successful in a good degree. It was then, and not till then, that he began really moving heavenwards. Before, he depended on states of feeling; but now on just acts to his neighbor, grounded on a religious principle.

XXXIII.

THE TWO PICTURES.

"How beautiful!" And the two men paused before the window of a print-seller.

The picture which had called forth from one of the men this admiring exclamation, was a showy bit of landscape, painted for effect, and well calculated to deceive an unpractised eye.

"I must inquire the price," said the speaker, whose name was Godwyn, and he drew his companion into the store.

"What do you ask for that landscape in the window?"

"Fifty dollars," replied the picture-seller, "and it's worth a hundred. But the owner wants money, and must sell, even at so great a sacrifice."

"Who is the artist?"

A name not familiar to either of the men was

given. But, as they were only posted up in art-news indifferently well, and did not care to make their ignorance known, no further question was asked. The name was accepted as belonging to an artist of celebrity.

"I must have that picture, Martin. It is a gem." Godwyn spoke aside to his friend.

"We have a companion piece by the same artist," said the picture seller, whose ears, all on the alert, had overheard the remark.

"Indeed! Let us see the two together."

The paintings were placed side by side.

"Charming!—beautiful!—exquisite!" were the exclamations with which their exhibition was greeted.

"I will take one of them," said Godwyn. "And you the other." Looking towards his friend Martin.

"I don't know about that," answered the latter. "The pictures are certainly very tempting. But I am not just sure that I can spare fifty dollars to-day for an article of simple luxury."

"They're cheap as dirt," said Godwyn. "Better take one. You'll not have another chance like this soon."

But Martin hesitated, debating the money-question involved, and finally decided to let the companion-piece remain where it was for the present. Godwyn paid down fifty dollars, and ordered one of the pictures sent home.

The two men left the picture dealer's and walked on, Godwyn elated by his purchase, and Martin well satisfied at having successfully resisted the temptation to spend the sum of fifty dollars for a painting, when he had other use for his money.

"You will regret not having bought that picture," said Godwyn. "It is a gem, and is offered at half its value."

"I love pictures," was answered. "They are to me a source of unalloyed pleasure. But my income is yet too limited to permit an indulgence of this taste. The common wants of life, and the charities which may not be disregarded, keep me without a surplus to expend in the merely ornamental."

"I am no better off than you are," said Godwyn. "But a portion of my income must go in the direction of beauty and ornament. Bare walls are my abhorrence"——

At this moment a cry of warning reached the ears of the two men, and looking forward along the street, they saw a horse, attached to an empty wagon, dashing towards them at a frightful speed. A little way in advance stood a cart, backed up to the pavement. Before the owner of this, an Irishman, had time to turn his horse, the runaway was upon him, and one of the shafts striking his poor beast on the head, killed him on the spot.

"Poor fellow!" said Martin, in a tone of pity, as he heard the Irishman bewail his loss.

"Come," said Godwyn, drawing upon the arm of his friend. "It's a mercy for the poor, half-starved beast."

But Martin stood still, and began to ask the Irishman questions. His looks corroborating his replies, satisfied him that the loss he had just met was the loss of means for getting bread for his children. The man was in deep distress.

"I can't wait here," Godwyn spoke, with some impatience. "Come, or I shall have to leave you. That picture will be home before I get there."

"Go on, then. I must look a little further into this case," said Martin, quite in earnest.

"Humph! You'll have your hands full if you stop to look into every case of this kind." Godwyn spoke a little contemptuously, and then went forwards.

"Ah, Martin!" said he, as the latter entered his store about two hours afterwards, "How comes on your Irishman and his dead horse?" There was an amused expression on his face.

"Badly enough at present," was answered. "Poor fellow! The death of his horse is to him indeed a calamity; like the burning of a mechanic's shop with all his tools; or the sinking of a merchant's ship, wherein was all his fortune. But I think we can put him all right with the world again, and at a very small cost to ourselves. I propose that five individuals contribute ten dollars each, and buy him another horse. Here is the list, I have put down my name, and Gregg has followed suit. You will make the third, and I know who to calculate on for the fourth and fifth subscriptions."

Martin only partly unfolded his subscription paper, for a strong negative came instantly into the face of Godwyn.

"I'm too poor to make ten-dollar subscriptions for the purchase of cart-horses for beggarly Irishmen," he answered. "If I once undertook that business, I would soon have my hands full. Take my advice, and keep your money, your time, and your pleasant feelings, and don't waste either in the thankless task of collecting money to pay for dead horses."

But Martin, though disappointed, was not turned from his good purpose. He succeeded in getting thirty-five dollars subscribed, and then, adding fifteen from his own purse, he went to the humble abode of the poor Irishman, whom he found, half stupid with despondency, amid his sorrowful wife and children.

"Come, come, Jimmy Maguire?" he said, cheerfully, "this will never do. Brighten up, man!"

"There's no brightening up for me, yer honor," replied Jimmy, sadly. "Poor Barny is kilt dead," and he drew his hand across his eyes. "The cart's of no use now, and if I was to die for it, I couldn't find money to buy another horse. Och! yer honor, and what is to become of us all?"

The picture that Martin looked upon in that humble abode lay all in deep shadow. There was not upon it a single gleam of sunshine.

"What did Barny cost?"

"I paid thirty-five dollars for him, hard-earned money, and he was chape at that, yer honor."

"Find another horse as good, or even a little

better than Barny, and I will buy him for you, Jimmy. Some kind gentlemen have placed money in my hands for that purpose."

Broad dashes of sunlight fell instantly on the living picture, which lay a moment before in deepest shadow.

"Oh, sir! Is it indade as you say?" Jimmy caught the arm of Mr. Martin, and looked into his face almost wildly.

"Just as I say, Jimmy Maguire. Find the horse, and I will make him yours."

From the valley of grief and despair to the mountain-top of joy, the Irishman's household passed, as by a single stride. They overwhelmed their benefactor with noisy gratitude, and placed him at once high in the calendar of saints.

That evening Mr. Godwyn sat alone in his parlor. The picture was on the wall, but his eyes were already more than half satisfied with its beauty, and ceased to turn themselves towards it for pleasure. A friend had been invited home at tea time to look at this picture. He had an artist's eye, and knew a good painting from a bad one. Unfortunately for Mr. Godwyn, he detected glaring faults in the landscape, and did not hesitate to pronounce it a fourth-rate affair, and dear at the price which had been paid. Mr. Godwyn was unhappy.

On the same evening sat Martin alone, gazing at a picture, the sight of which gave him inexpressible pleasure. It was not hanging upon the parlor walls, inclosed in gilded frame, but grouped in his thought, and vivid as life itself. We need not describe this picture. The reader knows that it represented the poor Irishman and his delighted family. Imagination had painted it in richest colorings, and memory was enshrining it in perennial beauty. There was no power in time to rob that picture of its charming freshness. Its possession could not bring a reproving thought; no critic was skilled enough in art to find a defect, and thus lessen the owner's appreciation. It was worth a thousand such pictures as the one his friend had already ceased to value.

The lesson, reader, is for us all.

If we were as ready to hang the chambers of our minds with beautiful pictures, as we are the walls of our houses, what pleasures would we lay up in store for the time to come. As we grow older, we insensibly fall into the habit of looking inwards.

We see more with the eyes of the mind than we do with the eyes of the body—oftener gaze upon the pictures that cluster on memory's walls, than upon those which hang on the walls of our dwellings. Oh! let us then give beauty and happiness to the future by daily acts of kindness—by tender charities—by deeds of human love. These will group themselves into pictures, upon which, as years glide away, and the eyes look more and more inwards, we shall gaze with purest delight; for time cannot deface them, neither will familiarity rob them of a living interest. And these are the pictures which are not left hanging upon walls that shall know his presence no more, when a man lays down the burdens of natural life. He takes them with him, as he takes the precious silver of divine truth, and the fine gold of celestial love; and they will help to make beautiful the mansion prepared for him above. Good deeds are the stepping-stones to heaven.

XXXIV.

TEMPTATION.

"If it wasn't for temptation," said a young convert, speaking to one who had been many years trying to walk in the narrow way, "I could get along very well. But the enemy is always taking me at unawares. I start out in the morning, resolved that my walk and conversation shall, in all things, adorn my profession; but ere I am half through the day, temptations assail me, and I fall."

"I trust not, my young brother," was the gravely spoken reply. "To *fall* in temptation is a most dreadful thing. Every man who is regenerating falls *into* temptations. Without them, we could not know the evil qualities of our hearts, nor be able to rise above them into the life of good affections. 'Count it all joy,' says the Apostle James, 'when ye fall into divers temptations; knowing this, that the trying of your faith worketh patience.' And again, he says: 'Blessed is the man that endureth temptation.' It is by means of temptations that spiritual life is formed, and through the conflicts that temptations bring that this life gains manly vigor. It is not falling into temptation that harms us, but falling in temptation—not the conflict, but the loss in battle. We must conquer, if we would have peace and rest. Can you not see that, my brother?"

"I see it," was answered in a troubled voice. "But your words form themselves into sentences of condemnation. Alas! I fall in every temptation."

"Do not hastily write bitter things against yourself," was the encouraging response to this. "Perhaps it is not so bad. If you will confide to me a day's experience, perhaps I can give you some aid, and some encouragement."

"Most gladly; for I am in need of help. This morning, before I left my room, I prayed most fervently that I might be kept stainless through the day—that a guard might be set upon my lips, and that all my actions might do honor to His name. Conscious of my own weakness, I wished to depend on Him solely; and so prayed, that He would substitute His strength for my weakness. Thus armed, as I thought, I went forth; but, ere the first hour had passed, I fell. A sudden assault upon my feelings was repelled by sharp words, instead of a meek reply; and so I dishonored my Lord."

"Will you state the occasion?"

"It happened in this wise. I was attending upon a customer who was captious and troublesome. She annoyed me greatly by some of her remarks. At last she called my word in question, which threw me off my guard, and extorted an angry response. Of course, she got angry in return, and left the store. It made me unhappy for the day. Next, I was betrayed into light and trifling conversation; and next, so far forgot myself, as so indulge in evil speaking and uncharitableness. Then I would discover that my thoughts were running on worldly and forbidden things; and once, I actually caught myself working out a secret scheme for overreaching in trade. I was so shocked at this, that I felt almost like abandoning my Christian profession. Isn't it dreadful to think of? I believed my heart changed; but now am sorely afraid that

I am worse instead of better. Oh, these temptations! Why is it that we are subjected to them?"

"It is by temptation that our evil quality is revealed to us," was mildly answered. "Now, as I regard your experience during the day, I think you have reason to be thankful for the occurrences which have shown you that there are things in your heart which must he removed ere you can advance in the regenerate life?"

"But, I fell in temptation," said the young man, in a troubled tone of voice.

"I am not so sure of that. Temptation is an allurement to sin—and sin is some violation of God's law; and we *fall* in temptation, when the right and the wrong are both clearly presented to our minds, and in freedom to do the right or the wrong, we do the wrong, because our natural affections love it. Now, let us try your actions to-day by this rule. First, as to the angry words to a troublesome customer. Would you have said them, if you had taken time for reflection?"

"No. I was pained the moment I gave them utterance."

"Enough; the pain showed the spiritual vitality. If you had felt pleased at having wounded or annoyed the person, the case would have been different; and if you have resolved to be still more guarded in future, the lapse on this occasion is only a stepping-stone, as it were, to better conditions of mind. Both you and the lady, it strikes me, will gain something by the incident. And let me help you to look a little deeper. Which gave you most pain, a consciousness of having wronged the lady, or of appearing unmanly in her eyes?—of having sinned before God, or of having disgraced yourself before men? Get at the truth, if possible."

The young convert turned his thoughts inwards, in close self-examination.

"You have helped me to look deeper,"—he lifted a pair of sober looking eyes to the face of his friend—"but I do not like what I see."

"Why?"

"It was not the sin that really troubled me. I thought more of man's estimate than God's."

"Which was wrong."

"Oh, yes."

"So much really gained by this loss of temper. Can't you see that the trial was for your good, and the fall, in a sudden assault, ere you had time to buckle on your armor, permitted, in order that you might be enabled to see deeper into your heart. You are on your feet again, and stronger than before.

"The next thing complained of, is light and trifling conversation; and the next, evil speaking; then your thoughts ran on worldly and forbidden things. Now, as to the light and trifling conversation, I have only to say, that religion does not bind a man to solemn, speech at all times, and in all places. Pleasant words are not evil, unless they involve some hurtful thing, as what is obscene, wicked, or profane—then they have a soul-destroying quality. Bring your conversation to this test always. As to the evil speaking, and pondering on forbidden things, they are to be repented of. If the discovery has pained you, that is another advance in the right direction. But, the most serious discovery you have made during the day, is the fact, that dishonesty lurks in your heart. Here was a real temptation, but, thanks be to God, who giveth us the victory, you were able to meet the enemy of your soul on the very threshold, and hurl him back with more than a giant's strength. Now, think for a moment, my young friend, and then say whether the experiences a little while ago complained of so bitterly, are not really day's stepping-stone towards heaven? Are you not wiser, and stronger than when the morning dawned? Is not the way plainer?

"Temptations help us onwards, if we but overcome in them; because they are revelations of our evil qualities, the existence of which we could not know without them. But if in the strife we fall, then we grow worse instead of better; then our steps lead downwards instead of upwards. Your morning prayer, to be kept from evil during the day, is well; but do not let the utterance of this prayer lead you to neglect watchfulness for a single moment. Prayer will not weaken your enemies, but render them, it may be, more determined and malignant. Watch through all the succeeding hours of the day, and keep your armor tightly girded. Be ready for sudden assault, or stealthy inroad; and then, as a true Christian warrior, you shall come off victorious."

"Thanks! thanks!" was the earnest reply. "You have helped me wonderfully. I see clearer, and feel both strength and encouragement. I have not really fallen in temptation, but am stronger for the brief conflicts."

"These," said the more experienced Christian soldier, "are but light skirmishings before the shock of battle. Your real temptations are in the future; but you will not be admitted to these until you have overcome the outposts and vanguards of the enemy. Then will come the fiercer struggles and wilder conflicts of the strong man. Now you have only the child's strength, and none but feebler foes are suffered to approach; but as you grow up towards the full stature of a Christian hero, the strongest and most malignant enemies of your soul will array themselves, and then you must conquer. Fear not; for divine courage and divine skill will be yours, if you go bravely into the fight; and when you have conquered, there will be rest and peace. Count it all joy, therefore, when you fall into divers temptations; for they are the trials of your faith, and the means by which you are enabled to put off the old man of sin, and to put on the likeness of the new man, Christ Jesus our Lord."

XXXV.

AT HOME.

A MAN'S "walk and conversation" at home give always the surest test of his profession. At home, few are dissemblers. The real quality manifests itself without disguise. If a man's wife, children, and servants, show no respect for his religious character, you may be pretty sure that he is self-deceived, or a hypocrite. In other words, that he is trying to get to heaven by a mere outside observance of pious forms, instead of through a denial of self-love, and the cultivation of heavenly affections.

Mortimer Grand had a very pious way with him. He was much inclined to conversation on religious subjects; fond of doctrinal discussions, and much concerned about his neighbors' fidelity in spiritual things. Most persons thought him a good man—some a *very* good man; but the few who came in closer contact, and felt the quality of his business life, held rather a different opinion. They saw that he was, for the most part, eagerly bent on securing personal advantage; and this even to the injury of others.

But it is in his home life that we design testing the religious quality of Mr. Grand. At home, shut out from the world's observation, he could lay off the assumed external, and act in all things just as he felt. If a tyrant in heart, he could act the tyrant; if impatient at light annoyances, he could be impatient; if inclined to selfish appropriation, there was none to prevent his doing as he pleased. He could enjoy the luxury of being himself, from inmost affection to uttermost act.

The day had closed, and in no very good humor—for all things had not shaped themselves as natural affections desired—Mr. Grand bent his steps homewards. On the way he met a friend. They stopped and exchanged salutations. Mr. Grand's face became almost radiant with smiles as he responded to the remark—

"The good work goes bravely on."

"Bravely and gloriously!" was his reply. "It is, indeed, a time of refreshing from the hand of the Lord. The signs of His presence are everywhere."

Then they shook hands with ardor, and parted. For a little way, the glow of enthusiasm remained with Mr. Grand; then, as home drew near, the warmth of his feelings subsided; and by the time his feet were crossing his own threshhold, his state was entirely changed.

"No light in the passage, as usual!" he said, fretfully, as he closed the street door behind him.

Even as he spoke, the faint, yellow gleam of a match broke suddenly out of the darkness, and in the next moment the strong glare of a gas lamp blazed around him. It was the work of his wife.

"Humph! it's always so!" growled Mr. Mortimer Grand.

"Yes, it is always so," replied Mrs. Grand, her tone of voice in no wise more amiable than that of her husband.

"What's always so?" was demanded.

"Your temper when you come home."

This was severe; and Mr. Grand was irritated, rather than rebuked. So he went stalking up stairs to the sitting-room, and entered among the children like a cloud instead of a sunbeam. There was a sudden hushing of voices, and a shrinking away at his approach. In the large cushioned rocking-chair, sat little Frances, whose loving heart was always going out in search of love. She lifted her blue eyes to her father's face, as he approached her, with a half-timid, half-hopeful expression. But he merely swept her from the chair with his hand, and sat down without a gentle word or glance of affection.

Dear little tender thing! The roughness and the disappointment were too great for her. Tears came; sobs convulsed her tiny frame; and then passionate grief broke in cries upon the air.

"Take that child from the room!" said Mr. Grand, sternly, as his wife entered.

"What's the matter with her?" inquired the mother.

"It's more than I can tell. She's always crying about something. But, I won't have this din about my ears. It's intolerable."

Mrs. Grand took the child up in her arms, and pressed her head down against her breast, tenderly.

"What ails you, dear? Stop crying, and tell me." Mrs. Grand pressed her lips to the ear of her child.

"Papa." It was all the little mouth could say.

"Papa, what?" Whispered the mother.

"Papa hurt me," was answered, amid quivering sobs.

And that was just the truth; and just as the child felt it. She did not mean to convey to her mother any impression beyond the truth. Her little heart was hurt.

"That is not so!" And Mr. Grand started to his feet. "How dare you tell a lie!" And he moved rapidly across the room. The frightened child shrunk closer to her mother, and hushed her crying. Mr. Grand took hold of her slender arm with the tight grip of passion, and attempted to remove her; but Mrs. Grand would not permit this. She was not going to trust her precious little one to the tender mercies of an angry man, whose hard spirit had bruised hers from the beginning. The result of former contests with his wife, warned Mr. Grand not to persist now; and so, after scowling upon her for some moments, he turned away and went back to his seat in the large rocking-chair, muttering something in an undertone.

For ten minutes Mr. Grand sat without speaking, his chin drawn down upon his breast, and his countenance wearing a most repulsive aspect. Then he ordered one of the children to be still, in a tone of harsh rebuke. Ten minutes more of moody silence followed.

"If supper isn't ready soon, I shall go off without it." Mr. Grand spoke suddenly.

"You didn't say you were going out." Mrs. Grand arose and moved towards the door of the room. "If you had, I would have hurried tea."

"Supper ought to have been ready half an hour ago. I've said, a hundred times, that I wished my meals always ready by stroke of the clock."

Mrs. Grand went down stairs, leading Frances, who kept close to her side. Nearly ten minutes more elapsed, before everything was on the table. Ere half that time had expired, Mr. Grand had commenced walking the floor of the sitting-room with impatient footsteps.

"Father!" A voice and hand arrested his attention.

"Well, what's wanted?" Mr. Grand stopped and looked down with closer contracting brows.

"Lend me your knife, father, to sharpen this stick?"

"I shall do no such thing. You broke the last knife I had." And Mr. Grand pushed his little son away, who, made angry by the rebuff, crossed the room to where his older brother was writing out an exercise, and from sheer wantonness, born of bad feelings, pushed his elbow and caused him to spoil half an hour's work. This outrage could not be borne; the brother turned and struck him in the face. A loud cry followed, when the father, catching up the boy who had dealt the blow, punished him with great severity, and then sent him off, supperless to bed. He made no inquiry—stopped for no investigation; but meted out summary punishment, because that was in closest agreement with his feelings.

When the tea bell rung, at last, he went stalking down stairs, the children following in a wild scramble.

"Silence!" He demanded in a tone of stern authority, as he sat down to the table. A grace was then said, when, helping himself, Mr. Grand left his wife to help the children. The toast was a little burnt, and he scolded; his tea wasn't sweet enough, and he called for more sugar, with a frown; the butter didn't suit his taste, and he spoke so sharply about it to his wife, that tears came into her eyes. After eating, with a good appetite, Mr. Grand left the table, saying, as he did so, that he was going out and wouldn't be home until after ten o'clock.

"Henry!" Mrs. Grand arose from the table, and followed her husband into the passage.

"Well, what do you want?"

"I wish you could stay home this evening. I was going to ask you, particularly."

"Stay at home! What for?" Mr. Grand knit his very flexible brows, as he always did when not pleased.

"Edward is not getting on right at school. He hasn't had his lessons for a week or more, and says he can't learn them. I have tried my best to help him, but the lessons puzzle me. Now, Henry, if you would only give him a little time this evening you might save him from discouragement and disgrace at school. He says the teacher keeps him in every day, and threatens severer punishment if he is deficient to-morrow. I promised him that I would speak to you about it."

"I've punished him, and sent him to bed, for striking his brother," said Mr. Grand. "I don't wonder he isn't getting on right at school if he behaves as badly there as he does at home.

The fault, I apprehend, goes deeper than his lessons. I don't believe his teacher is so unreason able as he makes out."

"But hadn't you better look into the matter? I think Edward is doing his best. He must have been very much provoked if he struck his brother. He is not troublesome among the children. I wish you would stay at home to-night and look into this matter of his lessons. If there is any injustice towards him, who but his father is competent to protect him?"

"Oh, as to the injustice, I will take all the risk," replied Mr. Grand, indifferently.

"Then you won't stay at home?"

"I can't. I'm going to a missionary meeting."

"Missionary meetings may all be well enough," answered the wife, coldly; "but my opinion is, that your duty to-night is to look after the neglected heathen of your own home."

"Mary, I will not suffer this!" Mr. Grand spoke sternly. "I know my duty, and am alone responsible for its performance. I wish you would do yours as well. We should then have a better regulated household."

And he went out, shutting the door with a

heavy jar. Mrs. Grand sighed, as she walked back, with weary steps, to the dining-room, and took up, with a sad heart, the burden of her duties. Mr. Grand went to the meeting, in which he took a prominent part, and came away at its close with pleasant compliments in his ears, and a feeling of self-satisfaction in his heart, in having been an active co-worker in a great scheme of Christian benevolence.

Of this man's title to the name of Christian, let the reader judge. We have another and sunnier picture to exhibit, and so pass from the contemplation of one that can only excite unpleasant feelings. True religion always shows itself best at home; for here disguises are put aside, and the man is seen as he is.

"I wish father would come home." The voice that said this had a troubled tone, and the face that looked up was sad.

"Your father will be very angry," said an aunt, who was sitting in the room with a book in her hand. The boy raised himself from the sofa, where he had been lying in tears for half an hour, and, with a touch of indignation in his voice, answered,

"He'll be sorry, not angry. Father never gets angry."

For a few moments the aunt looked at the boy half curiously, and let her eyes fall again upon the book that was in her hand. The boy laid himself down upon the sofa again, and hid his face from sight.

"That's father now!" He started up, after the lapse of nearly ten minutes, as the sound of a bell reached his ears, and went to the room door. He stood there for a little while, and then came slowly back, saying, with a disappointed air:

"It isn't father. I wonder what keeps him so late. Oh, I wish he would come home!"

"You seem anxious to get deeper into trouble," remarked the aunt, who had only been in the house for a week, and who was neither very amiable nor very sympathizing towards children. The boy's fault had provoked her, and she considered him a fit subject for punishment."

"I believe, Aunt Phœbe, that you'd like to see me whipped," said the boy, a little warmly. "But you won't."

"I must confess," replied Aunt Phœbe, "that I think a little wholesome discipline of the kind you speak of would not be out of place. If you were my child, I am very sure you would'nt escape."

"I'm not your child: I don't want to be. Father's good, and loves me."

"If your father is so good, and loves you so well, you must be a very ungrateful, or a very inconsiderate boy. His goodness don't seem to have helped you much."

"Hush, will you!" ejaculated the boy, excited to anger by this unkindness of speech.

"Phœbe!" It was the boy's mother who spoke now, for the first time. In an under tone, she added: "You are wrong. Richard is suffering quite enough, and you are doing him harm rather than good.

Again the bell rang, and again the boy left the sofa, and went to the sitting-room door.

"It's father!" And he went gliding down stairs.

"Ah, Richard!" was the kindly greeting, as Mr. Gordon took the hand of his boy. "But what's the matter, my son? You don't look happy."

"Won't you come in here?" And Richard drew his father into the library. Mr. Gordon sat down, still holding Richard's hand.

"You are in trouble, my son. What has happened?"

The eyes of Richard filled with tears as he looked into his father's face. He tried to answer, but his lips quivered. Then he turned away, and opening the door of a cabinet, brought out the fragments of a broken statuette, which had been sent home only the day before, and set them on a table before his father, over whose countenance came instantly a shadow of regret.

"Who did this, my son?" was asked in an even voice.

"I did it."

"How?"

"I threw my ball in here, once—only once, in forgetfulness."

The poor boy's tones were husky and tremulous.

A little while Mr. Gordon sat, controlling himself, and collecting his disturbed thoughts. Then he said cheerfully—

"What is done, Richard, can't be helped. Put the broken pieces away. You have had trouble enough about it, I can see—and reproof enough for your thoughtlessness—so I shall not add a word to increase your pain."

"Oh, father!" And the boy threw his arms about his father's neck. "You are so kind—so good!"

Five minutes later, and Richard entered the sitting-room with his father. Aunt Phœbe looked up for two shadowed faces; but did not see them. She was puzzled.

"That was very unfortunate," she said, a little while after Mr. Gordon came in. "It was such an exquisite work of art. Is it hopelessly ruined?"

Richard was leaning against his father when his aunt said this. Mr. Gordon only smiled and drew his arm closely around his boy. Mrs. Gordon threw upon her sister a look of warning; but it was unheeded.

"I think Richard was a very naughty boy."

"We have settled all that, Phœbe," was the mild but firm answer of Mr. Gordon; "and it is one of our rules to get into the sunshine as quickly as possible."

Phœbe was rebuked; while Richard looked grateful, and, it may be, a little triumphant; for his aunt had borne down upon him rather too hard for a boy's patience to endure.

Into the sunshine as quickly as possible! Oh, is

not that the better philosophy for our homes? Is it not true Christian philosophy? It is selfishness that grows angry and repels, because a fault has been committed. Let us get the offender into the sunshine as quickly as possible, so that true thoughts and right feelings may grow vigorous in its warmth. We retain anger, not that anger may act as a wholesome discipline, but because we are unwilling to forgive. Ah, if we were always right with ourselves, we would oftener be right with our children.

"You will be at the meeting to-night, Marston?" said a man to his friend. They had stopped at the corner of a street, and were about separating.

"Oh, yes. I wouldn't miss one of these Wednesday-night meetings on any account. I enjoy them very much; and gain strength for duty. You will be there?"

"Of course; nothing but a matter of life and death could keep me away."

"Good evening."

"Good evening. Come early, Marston."

And the two men separated. Both had recently

joined the Church, and both were ardent in their new life, almost to enthusiasm.

On his arrival at home, Marston found that preparations for tea were not in a very encouraging state of advancement; so he said, in a cheerful way to his wife, who was going about with a baby in her arms—

"You must hurry up things a little, Anna. This is Wednesday night, you know, and I wouldn't fail being at the meeting on any account. Give Maggy to me. There; now your hands are free. I ought to have come home a little earlier."

The pale, weary-looking wife, smiled on her husband, as she handed him the baby, and said, pleasantly—

"You shall not be late, dear. I will soon have all ready. My head has ached badly all the afternoon, and this has kept me behindhand.

"I'm sorry for that, Anna. Does it ache still?" The husband's voice was full of kind interest.

"Yes; and I feel unusually weak. The first warm weather of the season, always tries me, you know."

A shade of concern came over the face of Mr. Marston, as his eyes followed the retiring form of his wife. He was an industrious young man, with only a small salary; and his wife was trying to get along without a domestic. They had two children—a little boy four years old, and Maggy, the baby, who had not yet completed her first year.

In a shorter time than the husband had expected, his wife's pleasant voice called him to supper. He gave her the baby as he entered their little dining-room, and she sat down with it in her arms to pour out the tea.

"Does your head ache still?" inquired Marston.

"Badly; but I think a cup of tea will do me good."

"I hope so, indeed. Give baby back to me. I can hold her." And the husband reached out his hands for little Maggy, who, pleased to return, almost leaped into his arms.

"You must take her back, mother," said Marston, rising from the table, in about ten minutes, and reaching the baby to his wife. "It is late, and I must be away, or the prayer-meeting will open before I get there."

"But Maggy, who was very fond of her father, did not wish to leave him; and so struggled, after her mother had received her, and cried to be taken back.

"Papa must go, darling." Marston bent down and tried to soothe the grieving little one. As he did so, Maggy got her arms around his neck, and held on tightly. It took quite an effort to remove them.

As Marston shut the door of his dwelling behind him, and commenced walking rapidly away in the direction of the church, at which the prayer-meeting was to be held, he was conscious of an unpleasant pressure upon his feelings. What did this mean? He began at once searching about in his mind for the cause. At first, he could see nothing clearly; but gradually thought went back to the home he had just left, and to his pale, weary-looking wife and children, grieving because he had left them.

"Is this right?" The question came suddenly upon him, and almost arrested his steps.

"I am sorry to leave them alone to-night," he said within himself; "and wouldn't, except for the prayer-meeting. I gain so much strength and comfort in this means of grace, that I feel as if it would be wrong to neglect it."

And so he walked on, but with slower steps, his thoughts still returning to his home, and imagination giving more and more vivid pictures of his wife and children in grief for his absence. At last he stood still.

"I need the blessing I had hoped to receive this evening. The strength, the comfort, the peace," he said, still talking with himself. "But, poor Anna! It is hard for her to be left alone. And she isn't at all well."

"I will go back." He spoke out resolutely, at last; and commenced retracing his steps. "I must not consider myself alone. Perhaps God will give the strength and comfort I need, even if I do not meet to-night with his people."

"Oh, James, is it you?" Mrs. Marston started at the unexpected appearance of her husband, who saw, as she looked up, that her eyes were wet. "Have you forgotten anything?"

"Yes," he replied, as he stood gazing with unusual tenderness upon her.

"What is it? Can I get it for you?"

"I forgot to stay at home with my wife and children," said the young man.

"Oh, James!" Tears gushed over his wife's face.

"And I've come back to remain with them."

Mrs. Marston leaned her aching head upon her husband's shoulder, and sobbed. This unexpected circumstance quite broke down the little self-composure that remained.

"Did you feel lonely?"

"Lonely, sad, and discouraged," she answered. "But you are good and kind; and I am weak and foolish. Gò back, James, to the prayer-meeting I shall feel better now."

"No, darling," said Marston. "I will stay at home to help and comfort my lonely, sad, and discouraged wife; and I think I shall be serving God in this, with a truer spirit of worship than I could possibly feel in any prayer-meeting that I went to at the sacrifice of a clear home duty."

"How does your head feel now, Anna?" was asked half an hour later, as they sat together, Mrs. Marston with her needle in her hand, and her husband holding both of the happy children in his arms.

"It is free from pain, and I feel so much better. I think your unexpected return has cured me. Ain't I a weak, foolish woman, James? But, after you have been absent all day long, I can't bear to have you go out in the evening. I love so to hear you read to me; and you don't know how much good it always does me."

Mr. Marston smiled back upon his wife a loving smile. New thoughts were awakened in his mind.

"There are other souls to be cared for as well as my own," he said, a little while after, as he sat musing on the occurrences of the evening. "The souls of my wife and children. How can I help them on the way to heaven? By going out to religious meetings, or by staying at home with them? Ah! My duty is clear. I must *do* right before I can *be* right. If I endeavor to water the souls of others, God will water my own soul. He has placed these precious ones in my care, and I must be faithful to the high mission."

To think right is the first step towards doing right. While his wife sat at her work, Mr. Marston put his little boy to bed; first talking to him about heaven, and its pure inhabitants, and then hearing him say his prayers.

"God bless you, my son!" he said in his heart, as he laid on his pure lips the good-night kiss.

Another new thing in the household of Mr. Marston occurred that evening. As his wife sewed, he read to her, first from religious books, and then from the Bible. When bed-time drew near, he said, in a serious, but gentle voice—

"There are home prayer-meetings, as well as church prayer-meetings; and God has said, 'Where even two or three are gathered together in His name, there He will be in the midst of them.' Shall we not open a prayer-meeting in our house, Anna—a home prayer-meeting? There are two of us here, and God has declared that even with two He will be present."

"I am not strong enough for duty, Henry. Every day I feel that human strength is but weakness. Pray with, and pray for me, that divine strength will be given."

Mrs. Marston spoke with glistening eyes.

Then they knelt down together, and opened a prayer-meeting in their home; and Marston gathered in the act more strength and comfort than could possibly have been found at the public meeting, had he gone there in violation of his home duties, and sung and prayed never so fervently; for right actions, from religious principles, alone bear us heavenwards.

XXXVI.

WILD OATS.

THERE are steps away from heaven, as well as towards heaven, and a warning word cannot be wholly out of place, and so we give this earnest admonition to the young and thoughtless, and pray them to keep their minds pure.

Many a young man has been lured from the path of virtue, and enticed into the road that leads, by an easy descent, into the accursed valley of destruction, through the thoughtless speech of some thoughtless person, talking flippantly about sowing wild oats, as a thing to be expected in youth.

"I had one lesson on this subject from the lips of an aged counsellor," said a valued friend to me, not long since, "which has never been forgotten. The timely warning saved me. I was nineteen years of age, and had just entered college. Young men were there from nearly every State in the

Union, and some of them already sadly corrupted. I was social, in high health and spirits, and with an imagination forever carrying me beyond the actual and the present. Before I had time for reflection, and before even a consciousness of wrong had reached me, I was afloat on a dangerous sea, my boat gliding swiftly forwards, and the Siren's songs already in my ears.

"One night we had a wine party in the town, which ended in excesses, the thought of which has called a burning blush to my cheeks a hundred times since. I had not been very well for some days previously, suffering from constant headache and low febrile symptoms. The dissipation of a night turned the scale upon the wrong side, and I was so ill the next day, that it was thought best to call in a physician. He was an old man, of the old school of gentlemen, and wise, thoughtful, and kind. He commenced, at once, the business of finding out everything in regard to my habits, principles, and modes of thought, and there was something in him that so inspired me with confidence, that I concealed nothing. He looked grave, and offered a remonstrance.

"'Oh,' said I, almost lightly, 'young men must

sow their wild oats. The ground will be so much the better prepared for seeding wheat, after the crop is taken.'

"'An error of the gravest character,' he replied, seriously, 'and one that has ruined its thousands and its tens of thousands of young men. Is a garden, better prepared for the reception of good seed, for having been first permitted to grow weeds? I put the question to your common sense. Are there not some soils so filled with all manner of evil seeds, that the gardener, with his utmost toil and care, can scarcely remove the vigorous plants that spring to life in the warm sunshine and rain? It is no mere comparison, that of the human soul to a garden. It is, in reality, a spiritual garden. Truth is the good seed which is sown in this garden, false principles the evil seed, or 'wild oats,' which the enemy's hand scatters, if permitted, upon its virgin soil. Now, is it not as much an insult to reason to say that the man will be a wiser, truer, better man, for having false principles, leading at once to an evil life, sown upon the ground of his mind in youth, as it is to say that a garden will be more thrifty in after years, for being first permitted to grow weeds?

"'My stranger friend! I have lived almost to the completion of life's earthly cycle, and have seen a sad number of young men lost to the world, lost to themselves, and lost, I fear, to the company of God's blessed angels, in consequence of that single false idea sown into the earth of their minds. Oh, cast it out at once! Keep yourself pure. Let right principles, chaste thoughts, noble purposes, manly aims, grow in your garden—not the accursed wild oats! Be temperate, prudent, virtuous, obedient to superiors, honorable, kind. Aim to be a man—not a sensualist. Govern yourself as a man, instead of letting passion, appetite, or any sensual desire rule you as a tyrant. Sow no more wild oats. You will find trouble enough in your after life with the seed already scattered in your fields.'

"The scales," said my friend, "dropped at once from my eyes. I saw that the good old physician was right, and that this cant about sowing wild oats involved one of the most dangerous fallacies into which the mind of a young man could fall. It was my last folly of this kind."

XXXVII.

THE ANGEL PAIN.

"Oh, if it wasn't for pain," said Mrs. Warren, "life would be, indeed, a blessing! But pain mars everything. It is pain, pain, pain! This is the heirloom which every one possesses; and the mind must accept the fatal legacy as well as the body."

And the lady sunk back with a sigh upon the pillow from which she had raised herself while speaking.

"An angel who never sleeps at her post, is pain," said a gentle voice, the low tones of which filled the room like a passing strain of music.

"A malignant, destroying angel!" Mrs. Warren spoke with almost angry excitement.

"A kind, wise, loving angel," was answered firmly, "ever seeking to save. No enemy, whether of the body or the soul, can approach the citadel of life without a sure warning from this faithful sentinel."

Mrs. Warren's only response was a groan, accompanied by a firm pressure of her hand against her side.

"Does the pain increase?" was asked in tones of sympathy.

"Oh, yes! It seems at each breath, as if a knife were passing through me."

"The doctor will soon be here, I trust; and from him we may hope for speedy relief."

"I am so oppressed!" said the sick lady, panting as she spoke. "It seems as if a heavy weight were crushing in my breast."

"You did not feel that in the beginning?"

"No. The pain came first."

"Warning you of danger. I am glad we sent so promptly for the physician. You dressed too thinly last night. Bare arms and neck! I said the imprudence would bring its own punishment."

"Was that the bell?" asked Mrs. Warren, raising her head and listening.

"Yes."

"Oh, that it may be the doctor! This pain is dreadful?"

The doctor entered in a few moments.

"You did not send for me a minute too soon," was almost his first remark, after examining into the symptoms of his patient. It was a case of acute pneumonia. Mrs. Warren, who was a fashionable woman, had attended a fashionable party on the night before, with arms, neck, and part of her chest exposed. The company was large, and the rooms oppressively warm. Imprudently, she sought an open window for fresh air. A sudden check of perspiration was the result, and inflammation of the lungs the final consequence. Pain gave timely warning of danger, and aid was promptly summoned. Skillfully applied remedies met the destroyer at the threshold, and he retired after a brief conflict.

"Thanks to the angel pain!" said the sister of Mrs. Warren, as she sat by the feeble convalescent. "Your precious life has been spared."

There was a faint, assenting smile.

"If she had not been true to her mission; if she had slept one fatal moment at her post, and permitted disease to pass in without a stroke of warning, the darkness of death would now veil the eyes of our sister, and our hearts be shrouded in mourning. And so I say, blessed be pain! It is God's merciful gift!"

"Wise counsellor! sweet consoler! What would I not give, dear sister Anna, for your clear-sighted eyes — your Christian philosophy — your divine faith—your acceptance, not only in my person, but in your own, of pain as a blessing!"

"In nearly all cases," was the low-voiced answer, "pain comes from a violation of either natural or moral laws. If the former, the body suffers; if the latter, the mind. And thus being warned of error by the approach of evil, we turn to the physician and are healed."

She paused, letting her meek eyes sink to the floor, and remained lost for some time in thought.

"And so mental pain is an indicator of mental disease!" said Mrs. Warren.

"Always," the sister answered.

"Always?" there was a tone of surprise in Mrs. Warren's voice.

"But what if the pain arise from another's act, instead of our own?"

"As when the body receives external injury, for instance?" said Anna.

"Yes. Is the pain from mental disease in that

"Is the body in health when a hand is crushed, or the flesh bruised?" asked the sister.

"No."

"And sudden pain gives warning of the sudden injury. A condition of health no longer exists, and death may as surely follow without the physician's aid as if every pore of the body had absorbed contagion. As it is with the body, so is it with the spirit. One is materially organized; the other, as I have often said to you, is spiritually organized; and both are subject to laws which cannot be violated, even in the smallest particular, without evil consequences. It matters not whether the disturbance of harmony come from without or from within—the indicator, pain, gives surely its alarm, and ceases not until the danger has passed. If it were not so, spiritual death, which is the extinction of all good affections in the soul, would as certainly follow spiritual disease as natural death follows natural disease."

"I see, but dimly," said Mrs. Warren with a sigh. "Disease—pain—death! Alas! alas! There is not a human flower untouched by their blight. As for pain—pain of mind, and pain of body—it is the death's head grinning at all our feasts."

"Say rather, dear sister, the angel who points to the enemy of our peace, and cries, 'Beware! beware!' Look down into your heart, and question it closely. From what causes have arisen pain ot mind? From orderly or disorderly activities? That is, from neighborly and divine affections, or worldly and selfish affections; for in these two lie all the elements of life. There is not an impulse of feeling, nor the motion of a thought, lying outside of them. As the fountain is, so will the stream be. As the life is—orderly or disorderly—so will be the consciousness of life. The orderly movement will be smooth, harmonious, delightful; the disorderly, with shock, and jar, and pain.

"Dear sister, look into your heart, and answer the question—What has caused unhappiness? The activities of neighborly love, burning with a desire to bless others; or the activities of worldly love, seeking to receive rather than to bestow? Were we in the true order of our lives, we would be God-like, for we are the work of his hands; and to be God-like is to love others, and to seek their good. But if, departing from true order, we love only ourselves, and seek merely our own good, disease of mind follows as a sure consequence;

and pain, true to her mission, will give the needed warning lest we perish in eternal death. Mental suffering is, therefore, a sure sign that our life-motions are in the wrong direction. Pain touches us in mercy, not in wrath. Let us be wise, and heed her divine admonitions."

"The memory of a good deed," said Mrs. Warren, speaking from a new state of perception, "rarely gives us pain."

"Never," was answered, "when the prompting motive is good. But if we exercise neighborly charities from selfish or worldly ends, we cannot claim the high reward of interior delight. As our ends are, so always will be the quality of our enjoyments. Real good must be genuine, from inception to act."

"But how are we to know whether our motive be selfish or unselfish? Ends of life are most deeply hidden."

"We surround ourselves," replied the sister, "with an atmosphere so dusky that vision is often at fault. And so we move forwards, not always certain of our steps. But thanks to the prompter, pain, she will not permit us to swerve a hair's breadth from the right path, without giving a sign.

If we heed not her gentler admonitions, she speaks in clearer tones; and if we heed not yet, her voice takes on a harsher thrill. Louder, sterner, harsher it becomes, if our feet continue to walk in the ways that lead downwards; and she ceases not her cry, even unto the end. A blessing on pain, then, I repeat, dear sister! A blessing on pain! She is heaven-sent, and would lead us to heaven."

THE END.

www.ingramcontent.com/pod-product-compliance
Lightning Source LLC
LaVergne TN
LVHW020110110826
845151LV00001B/116

* 9 7 8 1 4 2 5 5 4 3 6 0 0 *